BETTER LEADERSHIP

HOW TO BECOME A DIFFERENCE-MAKER IN BUSINESS, YOUR COMMUNITY, AND FAMILY

My dear Cass,

I cherish you, admire you, and love you. For whatever relationship form we have, I am better for having known, trusted, and experienced who Cass is. Thank you for being you.

Always,

By

MARK MISSIGMAN

Chief Petty Officer US Navy (Retired)

BETTER LEADERSHIP
How to become a Difference-Maker
in Business, your Community, and Family

Mark Missigman Chief Petty Officer US Navy (Retired)

First Printing: October 2020

ISBN: 978-1-7358106-0-7

Mark Missigman
Mark Missigman Enterprises LLC
400 East Bay St
Unit 1704
Jacksonville, FL 32202
(757) 285-5508

www.MarkMissigman.com

Mark Missigman is available to be a speaker at your event and speaks on a variety of topics.

About Mark Missigman

MARK MISSIGMAN is a retired Chief Petty Officer of the US Navy, CEO and Founder of Mark Missigman Enterprises LLC, and an Executive Director with the John Maxwell Team. Mark is a keynote speaker, coach, and trainer for community and state organizations, and businesses.

His naval career spanned 20 years serving at sea, shore, and staff duty stations. He took part in the conflicts with Libya, Iraq I and II, Kosovo-Herzegovina; as well drug interdiction operations in South America. He was awarded the Navy Commendation Medal (1 award), Navy Achievement Medal (5 Awards), and Good Conduct Medal (5 Awards).

Mark Missigman Enterprises LLC is a leadership consulting company that serves small to medium-sized businesses. A thought leader company that can transform your business to a non-dependent high-performance culture. I can equip your staff, personnel, or team to perform what you want them to do; without you. You can stay out of the weeds of your business to focus on the most important part – more customers, clients, or patients.

You can access free resources at:
MarkMissigman.com

Table of Contents

CHAPTER 1
Why become a better leader? 1

CHAPTER 2
Leadership Defined – Your Brand of
Leadership 10

CHAPTER 3
You Can Do This...17

CHAPTER 4
Who are you?..29

CHAPTER 5
Who Can You Lead?...38

CHAPTER 6
What is the first step? 47

CHAPTER 7
You are Leading – Let's go! 56

CHAPTER 8
You have it going – What's next? 66

CHAPTER 9
Grow Other Leaders..77

CHAPTER 10
They Grow You..89

CHAPTER 11
A Story of Leadership 99

CHAPTER 12
Apply it to Your Life 118

CHAPTER 1

Why become a better leader?

Too often in our society, whether it be at work, home, or in the community there is a person in a leadership position that just does not measure up.

This lack of leadership, good leadership, has a detrimental effect on everyone that it touches. This is a major reason for failure, unhappiness, and lack of commitment. During these times, there are many opinions, accusations, and theorizing as to what the problem is. There is nothing worse than when we have tried our best but our efforts have not borne any fruit, or at least not enough to live on. The problems can usually be attributed to the top, the person in charge, the decision-maker or the leader.

In this book, I illustrate the problem, describe a solution, and offer a promise that, if you follow this process, you will become a leader that can achieve success, happiness, and commitment.

At work, it is the person at the top that should provide the leadership. But they may not provide the type of leadership to have a successful business. This can be the business owner, department head, or supervisor. In this type of environment many people, if not everyone, will only do the minimum required to keep their jobs. There is not anyone, or very few, who will go the extra mile to get the task done or do it excellently. There is often mistrust with leadership and among co-workers. The leader is more of the boss, rather than the person that the team relies on, e.g., the leader. When the boss enters the room or the workspace there is tension, uneasiness, and angst.

The same can be said for the person in charge at home. Is there constant fighting among the parents and children, or among the children, or among one child and one parent? It could be that one or more of the parents have poor leadership skills. However, in this book, I will not attempt to portray myself as a family expert, as my experience is only two families, my own, and my parents. But I will say that leadership in the home is especially important, as it creates a foundation for the culture of the family. It is very similar to leadership anywhere else, but it's harder. I say harder because of this saying, "familiarity breeds contempt". I am not sure who first said it to me but is attributed to the ancient writer in Rome Publilius, Pope Innocent III, and more recently Geoffrey Chaucer in his work Tale of Melibee, in the 1300s. The concept behind the saying, is that family knows you so well they know your faults and begin to only hear and see your faults.

If you doubt this, try to get your teenager to change the way they do things and see the results.

Think about a time when you may have heard a new singer or song, a new politician, or a new pastor at church. The newness of the music, lyrics, or sermon may have energized you. By contrast, an old song, pastor, or politician only seems to repeat the same old message. Familiarity breeds contempt.

We see problems in our communities when leaders are too narrow in their approach, are poor communicators, or lack vision. This confuses the members of the community and causes mistrust and despair.

My experience is with homeowner Associations, which are organizations that manage common areas of neighborhoods or housing complexes, like townhouses and condominiums. I have run afoul of these organizations in the past, by my actions and opinions. I have violated their rules by allowing mildew to gather on my rain gutters. In principle, I have no issues with these rules, but I do have issues with how they are communicated and enforced. Specifically, the mildew issue is on a property I rent out. I had not been to the property in about six months and, therefore, did not see the growth. Okay, maybe I should stop more often. But does that necessitate a letter from the HOA threatening involvement of a lawsuit? Whoa, I say, how about a letter or phone call that says: "hey we noticed this and want you to fix it in 30 days or less?" That seems more appropriate.

In our communities, leadership is vastly different and broader in the spectrum. Generally, I think it depends on what your goal or wish is. If you want to set an example for your community to follow, then it is more internal. The way to provide leadership is to act and interact with your community in a way to influence it. For example, if you live in the suburbs and you want to have a nice clean neighborhood, where the houses are well maintained then you must do the work on your own house. You must keep the lawn cut, green, and healthy. You must keep the outside of the house clean and sharp and in good repair. You should keep the trash to a minimum, keep the garbage cans stowed, and your car(s) clean or in the garage.

As you interact with the people in your neighborhood, be courteous, helpful, and respectful of their time and property. We all want to be seen as a nice neighbor. At least I do, and I am sure you probably do too. When we are positive in our interactions with others, it creates a good experience for them with us and brightens their day. When we are helpful to others, they appreciate it and we create the opportunity to lead them. Person by person, we can create a positive community.

If you want to be a leader in your community to affect change, then that is more external. What will your platform be? Will you be involved in a cause? Will you create a cause? Will you take a leadership position in a volunteer organization? If you choose any of these, your focus must be broader. Your focus must encompass what this cause is about, who is affected by it, and how the larger world affects it. You will have to set a vision for where you want the organization to go and then establish a culture for it to succeed. And you must develop followers, teammates, and leaders in the organization to help it succeed.

Better leadership is the difference. What do you see as leadership? The organization that has good leadership is winning. Think about organizations, like Chick Fil A. If you have ever been to one of their restaurants, you know the level of service you get when you are there. That is whether you are dining in or passing through the drive-through. In the dining room, there is always someone who comes to your table to ask if your meal was satisfactory and if you want a refill on your drink. In the drive-through, they are always pleasant, professional, and courteous. You always hear 'my pleasure' when you say thank you because it is their pleasure to serve you. They tout themselves as a service company that happens to have chicken, versus a company that serves chicken. This comes all the way down from the top. In John Maxwell's book The 21 Irrefutable Laws of Leadership, John tells the story of a leadership meeting he was invited to at Chick Fil A headquarters. The leader of the company, Dan Cathy was holding a leadership conference for his company and invited John to attend. This is what he witnessed: Dan Cathy was teaching -

"Now this is a nine-inch, 100 percent horsehair shoe brush. This is an industrial-strength shoe brush. It's the best you can get from the Johnston and Murphy Shoe Company. I'm going to present all of these, one to each of you here. And, John, why don't you come over here just for a moment. I made a commitment I'd never give one of these leadership relationship development tools to anybody without first showing you how to use it, so, John, step up here so they can see you here. And I'm going to challenge you to watch closely. This really has substance and real meaning when it's practiced with people that you really know, that you really work with a lot. So if you'll let me show you how this happens, I'll tell you how it works. Dan sat me down, kneeled at my feet, and began cleaning my shoes with the brush. Now this works whether the person's got tennis shoes, Nike, Reebok, it will work on any type of shoe, so don't worry about what kind of shoes the person has on. You don't say anything - that's one of the real keys here. And you're in no big hurry as you do this. Then [when you're done] you give them a big hug."[1]

This is service in leadership. This is why when you are Chick Fil A you know you are the most important person they will see that day. This is how they make you feel. Chick Fil A is only open six days a week and their competitors are open seven, but they outsell all of them. Does leadership make a difference? You bet it does.

Leadership has been around for thousands of years. If you know a little about history, even popularized history, you have heard of great leaders from throughout the ages. It includes names, such as Alexander the Great, Julius Caesar, Napoleon, and even Jesus Christ. Who created it, is a mystery. I guess that whoever had the biggest stick became the leader, or the best fighter, or who had the biggest army. But it has evolved as we have learned how to do it better, more effectively, and more humanely than beating someone over the head with a stick.

Leadership serves as a tool to help you get where you want to go, what you to want to achieve, and to find success. No one goes alone. You may be thinking there are self-made millionaires, self-made superstar

---

[1] John C. Maxwell. The 21 Irrefutable Laws of Leadership: Follow Them and People Will Follow You (10th Anniversary Edition) (Kindle Locations 705-710). Kindle Edition.

athletes, and self-made stars. I would challenge that thinking. Are they alone? Did they get that way solely based on their blood, sweat, and tears? One of the most recognizable people on the planet is Tiger Woods, a professional golfer. He does not have a team helping him make the shots that win him tournaments. Or does he? As you see on television, he has a caddy that gives him counsel on what to do and encourages him. I am pretty sure, like most professional athletes, he has a personal trainer, personal physician, chiropractor, and possibly a masseuse. This is not to mention his agent, lawyer, and accountant. He has a team.

How do you get a team? You get a team by becoming a good leader.

Leadership works when you get people to go along with you because they want to, not because they have to. You have made an impression on them. You have inspired them to follow you and they have bought into you. This applies to business, family, and community.

A surprising fact is that many people are looking for leadership. They want authentic leadership that they can get behind, they want help in thinking through things, and someone to help them make decisions. Some people doubt themselves, which is okay. But with good leadership, they become more confident in what they do and will do it better. You can make the difference for them. This is why you should want to lead them. It is for their benefit.

You can use it every day and in almost every situation. As we move through this book I will show you more about leadership, and how you can become a better leader.

Whether you want to positively influence your community or family, lead a successful business, or grow a dedicated team to help you meet your personal goals, you need to read this book. Your business will be more successful, have loyal teammates, and have the respect of colleagues. Your community will function better, find ways to solve problems and thrive. Your family will be happier, less prone to problems, and be loving. You will feel more fulfilled in your life.

CHAPTER 2

Leadership Defined – Your Brand of Leadership

What is leadership? How do you define it, see it, or know when you are doing it?

These are great questions. If we look at the definition of leadership in Merriam Webster, we find

1: The office or position of a leader

2: Capacity to lead

3: The act or an instance of leading.

These three examples do not help to bring clarity. Perhaps a better one is that "leadership is influence, nothing more and nothing less". This definition comes from John C. Maxwell, one of my mentors.

Forbes magazine contributor Kevin Kruse states that "Leadership is a process of social influence which maximizes efforts of others towards the achievement of a goal."

Both definitions use the word "influence". One is simplistic and to the point, and the other brings in the idea of social influence. My definition of leadership is "the ability to change thoughts or actions by others through agreement".

That is how we define it and use it through this book.

You can see it when people around you begin to follow you, speak like you, and seek your advice. You know you are doing it when you think of others first, what you can do for them, and help them with their lives, jobs, or relationships.

There are many great leaders that we can model, admire, and learn from. A few of my favorites today are John Maxwell, Simon Sinek, Darren Hardy, Carly Fiorina, and Pope Francis. These people are dealing with today's issues by leading with heart, compassion, and inclusion.

John Maxwell is the world's foremost expert on leadership, having produced more material on leadership than anyone in history. He has taught leadership in every country on our planet and has been invited to four Central and South American countries by their presidents to help reform their population.

Simon Sinek is a constant source of outside the box thinking and compassionate solutions delivered via books, podcasts, online conferences, and social media platforms.

Darren Hardy is a force in the personal growth and entrepreneur world. He is a purveyor of encouragement, wisdom, and practical tools to help you be successful in any business you want to choose. A disciple of Jim Rhon, Darren delivers his powerful messages via books, conferences, training, and webinars.

Carly Fiorina is a former CEO of Hewlett Packard and Republican candidate for President in 2016. Her candidacy was based, in part, on the platform of fixing Washington. Since 2016, she has committed herself to "fixing" Washington from the outside. She has held many leadership conferences, written books, and encourages thousands to live up to their potential.

Pope Francis, the pontiff of the Catholic Church which has 1.2 billion members, is an inclusive pope and leads with humility. Pope Francis has electrified the church and attracted legions of non-Catholic admirers, by energetically setting a new direction. He created a group of eight cardinals to advise him on reform, which a church historian called the "most important step in the history of the church for the past 10 centuries." Signs of a "Francis effect" abound: In a poll, one in four Catholics said they had increased their charitable giving to the poor this year. Of those, 77% said it was due, in part, to the Pope.

I look to these people for inspiration and guidance, as well as to my spiritual leader Jesus Christ. Like him, I subscribe to the traits of servanthood. A great leader is a servant of his people. As it says in scripture, Mathew 20:26 in the New Living Translation, "whoever wants to be a leader among you must be your servant."

I displayed this servanthood approach, when I was leading a group of 10 people on an assignment to support the United States Navy as a cyber security contractor. I was asked to lead these people who came from two different companies. One was my own and another our business partner. Another part of the challenge was that many of them didn't know each other or had never met. Some were brand new to the company, and me. And not all were from the same city or even the same region of the country. The task we had to accomplish was very stressful, as it had "top management" visibility and risk. Furthermore, the broader community of the command was not necessarily on board with the task, as they had resisted the move to a more secure network.

From Day One, there were challenges. Our task was to visit and secure every server across a 5,000-person organization where each department, division, or workshop had servers. The execution was also a challenge. We were only given a list of points of contact to call to make appointments. We were not given a list of servers or the specifics of each one. The servers were also spread out over a huge campus with multiple buildings, departments, and regimes.

Day One was about getting the team to gel. How do you do this when the team members were not only not from the same company but also were not from the same city, culture, or ethnicity? At first, this was daunting. I decided that we had to break down barriers, remove questions, and begin to get to know each other.

I had each person introduce themselves to the group. We all worked out of one room, which was a 10 by 10 conference room. Each member stated where they were from, what schooling they had, their certifications, if they were married, and where they lived now. I anticipated that this would begin to remove fear and doubt. Often, when people do not know about something, they fear it, therefore, I wanted to start the transition from unfamiliarity. This worked on Day One and, as time went on, people began to see where others were coming from and it allowed them to ask more questions and establish relationships.

Day One of execution involved me calling all the people on the list to make appointments for each team member to get the process started. I did this to set the tone for how we would approach the tasking and people – modeling the behavior to be emulated. The process for completing the tasking we had to make up, implement, and succeed with. Progress was slow at the beginning, but we soon began to get a rhythm.

Each of my days had one purpose, to ensure each member of this 10-person team had the resources necessary, software, tools, and task to be successful. This was my first and most important mission each day, even before I started on my assignments. I wanted to make sure they had something to do. There is nothing more demotivating than not having anything to do when you get to work. It is hard to keep your head in the game.

My servanthood leadership style helped the team gel together as a unit. On many occasions, team members volunteered to help each other out, stayed late, came in early, researched a problem to its conclusion, and, most importantly, began to care about one another. When one team member's family member passed. we all came together to help that person through the time. When one of us had a challenging customer, we offered to go along to see what we could do for them. We were constantly ahead of the schedule imposed by our customers, enjoyed group lunches, and argued the merits of android phones versus apple phones (androids are better).

In the end, we were remarkably successful, the command was able to pass their inspection easily, our customer was happy, the team was happy, and so was I. We had overcome many challenges over those four months, made great friends, accomplished many things, and proved that servanthood leadership works in tough environments.

The best evidence of the success of the group is that, although this task ended over 10 years ago, some of the members still keep in touch with each other. I have helped some of them get their next job, and they have touted me to other members in our career field. The best marketing is word of mouth.

CHAPTER 3
You Can Do This

You may be asking yourself, "Can I do this?" Or you may be telling yourself that you can't.

Well, you can!!!

I know that is a big statement. But I know you can. Because I know that you are the best in the world at being you. There are between 7.6 and 7.8 billion people on the planet when I write this. But you are the world's best at being you which, in turn, will make you the best at leading in your style.

Think about that. Out of every person, there is in the world, no matter what continent they come from, ethnicity they are, what education they have, or what family they came from, they are not better at being you than you are. You are the best, the absolute best.

As this relates to leadership, do you think being the best in the world at something gives you influence with people? You matter and your leadership matters, to change lives, change a direction for an organization, or to fulfill a need in your family.

These people need you to and you will make a difference to them.

I make this point because we, as humans (especially Americans), tend to compare ourselves to others. We often do this too much. But this only has a negative effect. I am not talking about evaluation, but comparison. When you look at another and think that you do not speak, look, or act like that, but you should. This is what I mean. Too often, as my friend and former coach Bobby Allen says, "we over evaluate and under celebrate." We need to turn that around, for your happiness, attitude, success, and, most importantly, for your leadership posture. You need to care less about what others are doing and focus on what you need to do.

As a leader, you must be the one that believes in himself, the goals, and the organization the most. As you try to influence people to follow, buy-in, and take action, they will be checking your belief in what you are asking. If they do not find a strong belief or conviction, their belief will not be very high. They are looking for inspiration, enthusiasm, and self-assurance from you that the road you are taking is the correct one. They want certainty, you cannot give them a guarantee, no one can, but you can give them certainty. That comes from you being your best. This is fundamental to your success as a leader. You must lead yourself well.

If you are wondering, worrying, or even have doubts about whether you can lead, consider this. Although I have had some success in the military, business, community, and family, it did not look so good at the beginning. I am the youngest in my family, a family of 12 siblings. That is right, my mother and father were married for over 50 years and during those years raised 12 children, of which I was the last. Well, technically my twin sister was the last, since she left home after I did, although she is 10 minutes older than I. (I am sure to remind her of that every year on our birthday too.) I have five older brothers and six older sisters. To say I was the runt of the family, is almost an understatement. The closest sibling in age was 5 ½ years older than us and he was not too happy to see two babies take his spotlight. I will save the details of retributions for another time. But, as it is in most boy's lives, there comes a time when you have to take your place in the world, in your house and your family.

This was the day for me:

"I was eight years old; I was at home; it was evening and I was watching TV. All of us who still lived at home were there, except for Dad. Mom, Susie, Liz, Matt, and Rachel, my twin. It was unusual for all of us to be home at one time, in the same room, and doing the same thing but we were. Dad was at work.

Susie was 17, Liz was 15, and Matt was 13 years old, and Rachel was 8 also, in case you were wondering. You cannot leave out the princess, even when it is obvious.

The TV was in the family room, and if you had ever been to our house on Mulberry St., you would know that room was not very big. It had two reclining chairs in it for mom and dad, and a couch or floor for the rest of us to sit on. The pathway to the room was between the couch and one of the reclining chairs. It was not very wide, if you sat on the end of the couch, you could reach across it to touch the person in the chair.

The pathway led to the kitchen. The kitchen was not much bigger than the living room. It had a table with six chairs sitting around and that was about it besides the fridge, a small closet, stove, and sink.

In the living room, Mom was in her chair, Susie was in Dad's, Liz, Matt and Rachel were on the couch. Matt was lying on the end nearest the pathway. I was on the floor because everyone else was a lot meaner than I am.

I think something happened during the stressful day, or Mom just had a long day. I remember she was tired. She proclaimed to us "Let's just sit, be quiet, and enjoy this show for a while." As good children, we wanted to oblige her to let her rest. We settled in to quietly watch TV. There were no cell phones, Play Stations, beepers, Game Boys, or any other such electronic devices back then. The TV was the only electronic device, receiving its stations over the air on rabbit ear antennas.

As the night went on, watching our program, I felt the need to get up to go out to the kitchen, to get a glass of water. No one else had said anything or moved for some time.

As I got up to walk through the pathway, Matt, being the big brother, hit me on the leg. He did not just hit me with a fist, he used a knuckle punch that was sharp, hard, and always left a bruise. He also yelled "Mom said sit and watch TV." Of course, I yelled back "I'm just getting some water." Mom said, "Let him go and stop hitting him." Sounds normal, doesn't it?

As I was in the kitchen, I was very mad at him. How can he do that when we are supposed to be quiet and be good? I was just getting water! And man, that hurt, his punch got me right in the thigh muscle and I was walking with a limp. As I was getting my glass of water, I vowed to get him back. I was going to stand up to my big brother. I was going to teach him a lesson to not hit me again.

I had a plan. I was going to go back to sitting on the floor, and at the next commercial I am going to get up again to go to the kitchen. As he lay on the couch, I could see Matt had his right arm under the pillow and used his left to hit me. When he goes to hit me with his left hand, I am going to knock it away with my left and sock him in the eye with my right. Yeah, that will do it, then he will know. He will be knocked out on the couch. I will be the victor! Yes, this was going to work. (At least I thought so, in my 8-year-old calculations.)

As I sat on the floor, waiting for the next commercial, I was excited. I do not think I heard a word of the show, as I was already reveling in my victory. This was going to be epic. I was never going to be picked on again. Today is the last day of that. This is a new day. I would be a champion soon.

The commercial came on. Here we go. As I got up, I can still see his face, getting mean, and yelling "sit down". I kept going, determined to claim my crown. Just as I predicted, he swung his left to hit me in the leg again. Just as I planned, I swatted that away leaving the left side of his face exposed to my thundering right fist coming down on his eye.

Boom!

I remember thinking, that didn't feel as good as I thought it would. I thought that probably hurt. Damn.

The house exploded. Everyone in the room could see what was about to happen, then it happened, and everyone yelled something all at the same time – Mom, Rachel, Liz, Susie, and Matt. I think I was yelling too but I was so scared, who knows what I was saying. I ran into the kitchen, all four steps it took to get there.

Everyone followed me out there, especially Matt who was hot on my tail. Luckily for me, Mom had a hold of the back of his shirt keeping him off of me, which was good because he probably would have ended my life right there.

The trial began. As Matt and I plead our case with Mom about who was more at fault than the other. Mom was playing mediator, and judge and jury, but I was not liking this outcome. My plan didn't factor this in. My punch was supposed to be the end. I was growing frustrated as my championship was slipping away from me. So I reached back for another crashing right to punch Matt again and finish him off. This was going to be it. Everyone will know I am the champion.

As I waited for this punch to land on target, I couldn't wait to claim victory. But, at this moment, Matt ducked and I hit Mom right in the face. Yes, you read that right, I hit her right in the kisser.

You could have heard a pin drop in the kitchen. All the air went out of the room. There was dead silence, and no one moved. I watched Mom flick her tongue to her lip and cheek to check for damage. She was okay but I could see her lip and cheek begin to swell.

The silence became deafening, as I saw my life flash before my eyes.

Susie broke the silence. "Mark, you are dead, when Dad finds out." She, for once, was right. I will be dead. Liz joined the fray as she and Susie began to argue about the last hours of my life. Matt was building his case of innocence, with Mom as his lawyer to Dad. I was thinking well, eight is pretty old, I had a good run, I wanted to play little league, kiss a girl, and drive a car, but I guess I will not get to do that. I hear heaven is pretty good, if I get to go. I might as well give my baseball cards away.

Dad will be home later that night. We were in trouble. Dad would always say when he left for work, "listen to your mother." And he would be mad if he got home to find out we had not. But hitting Mom was on an unimaginable crime. Even by accident, which I knew was not even remotely an excuse he would buy, no chance. I was on death row.

Then it came, Mom's calming voice. She had regained her composure from the punch that stopped the world. She said, "Everyone, calm down, go back and sit in the living room while I figure this out."

After a bit, she gave us the plan. It was a good plan, but would it work? My life hung in the balance. "Mark, you know how you play Nerf Basketball in the kitchen?" I said, "Yes, Mom." "Well, you were playing and jumping around as I was getting into the fridge, I was bending down to get something out of the bottom drawer. When I was getting up you came down and your elbow hit me in the face."

I loved this plan!!!

This could work! Susie was against this. She wanted to see the blood bath. The rest of us were with mom, whatever got us off of death row we were for.

Mom said, "Don't worry Susie, I am taking away Nerf Basketball for a week." Susie objected again. Mom said, "Too bad, that's it. It will work and no one, you hear me," as she raised her finger which we knew was law, "no one will tell anyone what happened. Or we are all in trouble. You get me?"

Mom affirmed with each of us our commitment to the plan. We all agreed. "Yes, mom."

The next day was judgment day. I knew I had to face Dad. The big question was will I crack under the pressure or would anyone else. As I entered the kitchen where he was having breakfast, I do not think I was breathing. I'm pretty sure I wasn't.

Dad said to me, sounding like thunder, or God's voice, "Mark, I want to ask you about last night." Holy crap, the fear of the Lord just went through me. I think I peed my pants a little. Here we go. Stick to the plan, stick to the plan I kept saying to myself. I looked at Mom, who said, "It's all right Mark, you can tell him."

So, I confessed the plan just as mom had told us, word for word as if I was reading from a script. I even acted it out to show him how it happened. The Nerf hoop on the closet door by the fridge, I jumped, and my elbow was out right next to the fridge. I showed it was truly possible. It was an Oscar-winning performance, even if I say so myself.

Then the miracle happened. He said, "All right, just be more careful next time and no Nerf Basketball for a week." He believed me.

Oh my God!!!

I was going to live! I was going to play little league, kiss a girl, and keep my baseball cards.

I looked at Mom. She winked at me, as she asked, "What do you want for breakfast?"

It was over.

Now please forgive me, I know that mothers hold a place of distinction in society, most do, that normally includes nurturer, caretaker, protector, and multitasking; lying is not usually on the list of positive motherly qualities. But this may be one exception to that rule.

Why did I relate this story? It is because up until that day, I lived in fear of my older brother. As I said, he was not too pleased to have his kingdom taken down by my arrival. He was only five, so I do blame him nor hold a grudge. But it was difficult to look up to him, only to be rejected over and over. It created a mindset of lacking, of unworthiness and lack of confidence. I am not sure if this relationship was the result or another but, as a kid, I had a speech impediment. I could not say my "S's". If you know much about these things, you will know that this is most often not the result of a physical ailment but an emotional trauma. Possibly over time, this was cultivated. I'd rather not try to find this answer but just be glad to have overcome it.

This, the day of my thunderous victory, was my day to claim my place in the world. It allowed me to believe in me again. It was the first day I realized I had the control in my own hands. Now, please hear me on this point. How I deal with problems at eight years old is not how I advocate dealing with them as an adult – I do not use my hands to make my point. I use my words. However, over my life, I had to face doubt, , overcome tragedy and fear, and live.

Believing in myself again, speech therapy, and the grace of God has allowed me to overcome my speech impediment. I know you have challenges too. We all do. But I know you, like me, will find your tool against your foe to become the best you, and leader, you can be. We need you to, the world needs you to because you have gifts no-one else has. You have people that will hear your voice loud and clear and say I have been waiting for someone to say that, be that, and do that. Oh yes, this is for sure. How cool is that? You will make a difference.

You cannot become the best leader you can be, without a strong and healthy self-belief. If you do not have that, how can you expect, demand, or receive that belief from someone else? There are reasons why people follow strong leaders. They see in them the strength they do not possess. You provide that for them, and they will feed off of that. When you look in the mirror you must have a confident, self-assured, but humble person looking back at you. It is someone who knows their strengths and weaknesses. You must know yourself.

CHAPTER 4

Who are you?

W ho are you? What is it that you do best? We need to answer these questions before we can move forward to be the best we can be. If you are self-aware and someone who has the talent, skill, and habit of self-reflection, these questions may be easy to answer. Whether you reflect regularly or not, you can benefit from an assessment of yourself to see where you are now. I would also recommend a personality assessment to better understand how you are put together; how you think, act, and behave. These assessments are very good at determining what is your make up. I have completed Clifton Strength Finders assessments, TriMetrix EQ emotional intelligence assessments, and DISC assessments. Strength Finders is a method to see your potential to leverage that into great performance, TriMetrix EQ helps you understand your emotional makeup, and DISC is personality indicator shows you how you are wired, communicate, and lead best. I found value in all of them.

I particularly subscribed to the DISC personality assessment. This assessment measures our ability to communicate, strengths, weaknesses, and our leadership ability. Your personality is then defined as Dominant, Influential, Steady, or Compliant (DISC). I was in a two-hour training conference session with Dr. Robert Rohm and, as he explained DISC to us, I misdiagnosed myself. Dr. Rohm did a wonderful job of explaining the four DISC personality traits as they related to people, scenarios, and real life. It was enlightening and informative. He explained the traits of the D personality, the I personality, the S personality, and the C personality. It was pretty easy to see the differences. Then he asked the audience to stand in the corner of the room that corresponded to what we thought our dominant personality trait was. We had a good time figuring ourselves out and, as many of us knew each other at this conference, we affirmed each other by saying "I see you as the S, that is so you." I chose the D personality as my dominant trait. As I was standing with the D's taking in the rest of the session, my friend Becky who was standing next to asked me, "You think you are a D, Mark?". I said,

"Yes." "That's funny, I find you more of an I, inspiring". Now, Becky is a fantastic coach and personal development expert, she is trained and coaches personal development in her business. So, I immediately considered her comment. It made an impact, but I had my thinking, makeup, and persona I was trying to project to the world. At the time, I disagreed with her, I said to myself "I am not inspiring." I stuck with the "D" choice.

As time went on and I began my education and certification to become a DISC Personality Behavior Consultant, the nagging question of what personality type I am kept bugging me. I had to know. So, as part of the course, I took my assessment. Even though at this point, I knew the basics of DISC and the types, I answered the questions of the assessment as honestly as I could. I made sure to choose the answer best suited to me and the one that came first or was my gut reaction. I felt this was the best way to assess the "real" me. When the assessment was over, my results were provided quickly.

To my surprise, and dismay, I was not a D personality but a I personality. My dominant personality was inspiring and influencing versus decisive and direct. Holy smokes! What did this mean? What is this saying?

This meant a lot of things. It meant on the surface, that I was not being myself. If I was not being myself, who was I being? As I talked about earlier, I am the absolute best at being me, but I was leaving me on the shelf! At least I was in my self-image. What did this cause? This caused confusion, I was thinking one way, as a D, but acting another, as a I, as Becky pointed out. (She was right apparently).

This caused confusion in my mind and in the people I was trying to lead. The confusion in my mind was that I did not understand fully the results I was getting. They did not match what I thought they should be. I had built a rationalization in my mind and adjusted my view, so I could survive and thrive. In a sense, I was adding an extra step of thought every day, for each scenario, task, or interaction. During my time of confusion, I struggled to decide whether I was doing my best. It did not feel like it. The pervasive fact I realize now is that I was holding myself back because I did not fully know myself. I was trying to play life left-handed, when I was right-handed.

It was difficult. Therefore, I implore you to take one of these assessments to be sure you fully understand you. I like the DISC, and I guess I am partial to it because I teach it in my business. But I like it for its simplicity and accuracy. I have had one client, Sarah, who says, "It is way too accurate."

The other reason I want you to know you is so you can be 100% confident as you lead. One of the main tenants of great leaders is their confidence. And that confidence comes from being finely attuned to who they are and what makes them tick. They do not try to be anyone else but themselves. And they are the best at being them. I want you to be a great leader and you can only do that when you know you.

Another great tenet of a leader, is that you are authentic. Authenticity comes from you revealing yourself to the people you lead. Let's face it, everyone can sense and identify a fake when they see and hear it. Except the one trying to be fake. And you do not want to be that person because they have a short shelf life and will not be leading for long. Authenticity has many benefits for a leader. It creates trust between him or her with the people they are leading. Authenticity allows them to buy into you. It allows them to see a real person behind the position, title, or office. They may even say "hey, she is like me." When you can invoke that in the people of your team, then you have earned the right or privilege to lead them. They will allow you to lead them. This is where the rubber meets the road and where you want to be. You can do this.

If you are having doubts, think about this. Even though I was thinking one way and acting another, it was my authenticity that kept my team together. One of my teammates, Paul, said during a conference call "at least he admits his mistakes." That's authenticity; and a little integrity.

At the time, I thought this was the only evaluation of Paul's comment. But I know realize that, because of my false thinking, I was sending a confusing message to my team. I was sending a combination of a D and an I, I was saying D things and expecting D results but was getting I results because of my behavior. As you may know, people will listen to what you say, but they will believe what you do. My team was watching me and acting accordingly. But I was making it hard on them. I was forcing them, unknowingly, to interpolate my words into my actions, because they believed my actions. This probably caused them some stress and anxiety trying to figure out exactly what I wanted. Their thoughts may have been "I heard what he said, but last time he rejected what I did, but accepted this, so I will do that." Has that ever happened to you with a boss? Or, are you that boss?

Please forgive me for using the word boss, I do not equate leader and boss. But for this scenario, I will use boss because I was communicating as a boss versus a leader. Because I was not communicating clearly, nor evaluating fairly. I am sure this frustrated some folks. Those who were confident and strong enough would push back and we would have conversations to agree. This was not devasting to the team, project, or success but I could do better, I realized. I should do better to allow even greater success.

You need to know you because you are the hardest person to lead. Yes, it's true. I know you may have immediately disagreed, or wonder what I am talking about, but we are the hardest person to lead because we judge ourselves by our intentions. Intentions are nice, but they are not the results. Let me give you an example. I try to promote myself, or look at myself, as a healthy person. I eat right, get enough sleep, exercise regularly, get chiropractic adjustments, acupuncture sessions, and all the things that one should do to be healthy. I will also tell you about these things, if we ever have the chance to meet and the subject would turn to health. If I am so health conscious, then how can I eat rocky road ice cream with chocolate chip cookies? Or stay up late binge-watching the latest series of my favorite show?

This is where my self-leadership in regard to my health fails. It happens the same way in my performance in business, relationships, and my community too. I fail at things, often. Additionally, I may not always recognize it. If the feedback is not immediate, I do not put on five pounds immediately from the ice cream, I may not acknowledge consciously that I must tighten up some things. Therefore, this is carried along with me as I go. My waistline will know. It is the same when we perform in our businesses, careers, families, and communities. Self-awareness is key to limiting the effect of this "blind spot" that we all have. But when you are aware of this blind spot, this makes you so much more effective. My blind spot is that I care so much about acceptance and others liking me that I may promise the world, but, as we know, I cannot deliver the world to anyone, not even myself. But I can help you in some way. Being aware of this blind spot, has allowed me to disappoint people less, make a more reasonable promise, and strengthen my ability to succeed. Even though my over-promising made me feel I was connecting with folks, when I didn't deliver that would hurt the relationship and I would feel the failure. This became an obstacle when it happened too often, or in a big way. I have become more attuned to understanding where this line is to not cross it, but also to continue to invest in the relationship. I am better balanced.

I want that for you. Know who you are, before you try to lead. At the end of this chapter, there is a resource to get you started. If you know who you are now, you lead better now. You will be glad you did, your teammates will glad you did, and you will have more restful nights.

Another thing, and the most important thing, you need to know about yourself is why do you want to lead? This is the most important question because it will determine how you lead, who you lead, and what your results will be. Do you want to make more money? Get to be the CEO? Be seen as powerful? Change the world? Change your address? Any number of motivations can be drawn from. I would not limit them but, whatever the motivation is, let it be pure, righteous, and serving.

Leadership is influence, as we stated previously, and you will see in the following chapters. Thus, what is the purpose of your influence? There have been many leaders in the world whose aim was not for the good, common good, or in serving those they lead. Some examples come to mind; Hitler is probably the best example and I apologize to mention such a horrific man. But I want to make sure you understand that leading people is a responsibility because you are interacting and touching people's lives. Your motives and purpose must be clear to you and you must be ready to take this on. You must understand that having people follow you is a task that you must not take lightly. I believe, if you have picked up this book, your motives are correct, on the proverbial straight and narrow, and for the common good of those you lead, now or in the future.

At BetterLeadershipbook.com, there is a short self-assessment to get your started to know more about you.

CHAPTER 5

Who Can You Lead?

Y ou may be asking that, and this is a great question. What do you think? I bet you have a few names on your list. I would also bet that a reason you may have listed is that you feel they need you. They need your leadership. Well, let me tell you, unless those people are your kids or dog, they are probably not looking for you to lead them. They would already have asked. But you are going in the right direction.

I know this may sound crazy. We have just a spent a chapter clarifying, deciding, explaining and defining who we are, so we can lead and you are ready to go. I know you are, and you are ready but first we must define your target. There are several factors to consider first.

There is the law of magnetism. This law states that you do not attract who want but you attract who you are. Surprise! This is why we took the time to define who we are, what we are and why we want to lead. Because your first followers, your first teammates, and kool aid drinkers are those like you. This law is explained in the New York Times Best Selling Book "The 21 Irrefutable Laws of Leadership" by John C. Maxwell. The law states as I said, "who you are is who you attract."[2]

This is okay. Do not be disappointed, because most of us start out this way. Additionally, this will make your first team more easily to communicate with and get along with. Because they will have the same traits as you. But eventually as you may know, someone who is just like will eventually reveal the same flaws, habits and weaknesses. For example, a team of folks who do not like details will not make good accountants. A team of folks who are shy will not make good salesman. Similarly, a team of people who do not like to cook, will be skinny or broke. I think you get the point.

When I look back on this from my own leadership journey, I realize that this really was an advantage. I

---

[2] The 21 Irrefutable laws of Leadership John C. Maxwell page 104.

found people like me, so I could try my leadership on them to spread my wings. I felt comfortable enough to try new things and they were comfortable enough to tell when it worked and did not work, without harming me.

I remember early in my naval career, I had gained some rank and was in a leadership position for the first time. I was excited and dreaming of taking on the world and being successful with my team. I had two people on my team. We were all about the same age, within a few years of each other. I went to them with excitement. I told them how good we were going to be, how we would together run the ship, and become a great team. Their response? "I do not want that. I am not excited about that." Ouch! My first motivational speech in my naval career was a colossal failure.

I made two mistakes. One was that these were not my people. We did not share the same values and I mistakenly felt they needed me by my own evaluation and thought. Not by theirs. And two was that I never considered or found out what they wanted, before laying my plan on them. Again, not my people.

So, who can you lead? Once you know all the answers from the previous chapter and are confident in them, you must set out to find them. They may not be far as the old saying goes "birds of a feather, flock together". But if you are new to understanding this part of you, you may have to take some time to look for them. They may also be the team at work or your business. And you will have to do the best you can, for now, as you did not assemble them. We will get those in a later chapter.

What are you looking for? You are looking for folks who have the same values that you have. Do you they believe mostly what you believe the way you believe things are done? Do they have the same work ethic? Is it the same sense of right and wrong? Do they like the Yankees or the Red Sox? No, this last question is not relevant but thought I would throw it in to see if you were paying attention. The correct answer are the Red Sox, by the way.

What you should do is look at what you value and make a list. Then observe yourself or ask someone you trust to observe you. If through observation, you perform, act, or behave this value, then you are assured this makes the list for finding this value in someone else. This means you have confirmed your value in you. Once you have vetted your values, now you have a solid list, you know you can attract this person by who you are, and they will be attracted to you.

Next, you must have a vetting process for people on your team. A good place to start is to figure out what do you need. If you are you starting a new business, then what position do you need or want to fill first? Let's say you are looking for a sales manager. Okay, what qualities do you think you need in a sales manager? Write those on your list. Then, as you begin to see people in your sphere of influence, in your network and in your neighborhood, it will become clearer as what person you will lead.

If you are working for a business or organization, you can do this too. There are people for you to lead. To be able to lead, you do NOT have to have the title of manager, supervisor or foreman. The person who leads is the first one to help. Are there people around who need a little help? Can you help them? A good start is to ask, "may I help you?" It is as easy as that.

What also makes it easier, is if you have a relationship with this person. You may have heard that success is built on relationships and leadership is no different. When you have a relationship with someone, when you know who they are, where they went to school, are they married, single, who they like in the game coming up or what is their favorite lunch time meal; then it makes it easier for you to lead them. Add your own curious questions to the list, make how you make relationships your own process.

What is the foundation of every relationship? Whether that is with a co-worker, a friendship, your pastor, your neighbor or your doctor. The foundation of every relationship is respect. Respect allows for two things; one is that you know the other person for who they are and two it allows for the exchange between two people to be void of manipulation. When two people have respect for each other, then the seeds of trust can flourish.

When you trust someone, you will hear them, and they will hear you. You will begin to walk in the other's shoes.

When you have earned another's trust and they have earned yours, you are ready to go. Now when you ask the question, "how can I help you?" they will think about it. They may also come to you to ask for help.

Now, you have the "privilege" to lead them, to be involved in their career and possibly in their life. I say privilege because it is a privilege to earn the ability and allowance to lead another person. You must think of it as a privilege that someone else is allowing you to speak into their career, job, and life. Taking this position is cherishing and valuing people. This is leadership on the high road, the best way, and the way that values people.

You should look for people who are motivated; they are doers. They are the ones who usually are in constant motion. They are getting things done and are engaged with what is going on in your business. They are people who you see are going the extra mile to serve your business, organization, or customers. Also, these people are displaying those values you listed. Of course, you must get to know them first, as I said have a relationship with them, so you can communicate with them on a level beyond the perfunctory conversations around the water cooler. If they are outside your organization and you are hiring them seek out people who know them to determine their worthiness or value to your company.

You will be able to lead those people that you have gained respect and trust from. You may be thinking that takes time. You would be right. But how else would rather do it? By manipulation? Fear? Those tactics do not have good results and no long-term return. People who lead by these methods will leave the company; people know when things do not feel right. You may be able to fool them for a time and think you have this licked. But they will figure things out and find another place to work. People do not leave companies, they leave people.

Do you want to have a company where people work there for a long time or even life or a revolving door?

You want to find the person that will spend his/her time researching for a solution to a problem. My team and I were supporting a Navy program that provided navigation autopilot for ships. We were engineering and implementing cybersecurity technical solutions for the system. In an effort to be efficient and provide the best service to our customers we devised a plan to have the entire team on site in the test facility, rather than one or two to implement and test several times, then eventually have a whole solution. Our plan was to research, test, and evaluate in our lab and then just come to implement in the test facility. We figured this would the best use of the time and shorten the schedule. It all made sense to us and the customer.

So, we arrived Day One on Monday to complete this by Friday, the schedule demanded it. We got to work straight away, all five of us were vigorously working to configure technical settings into the million dollar automated navigation system. The plan was to implement some of the solution, then test at the end of day one to ensure we had a working solution. Well, we did not. We have banked on this working and were certain that it would. To say we were heartbroken, is an understatement. And I was worried. It cost a lot of money on travel expenses for five of us to do this trip and a lot of professional credibility was used to gain buy-in for the plan. There was much to lose, including our reputation, trust, and maybe the contract for the work. As I pondered what to do as the leader of the team, one of my teammates suggested, "let us take tonight to let me do some digging on the internet to see where we went wrong. If I cannot come up with something, if not then we can break it to the customer tomorrow and find a new way." Our backs were really against the wall because the program schedule was set, and we did not have much time. I said "Okay." The next day, this teammate came in with the plan, it made sense and he had a quick test to determine its viability. He made the changes, did the test and it worked. We were saved, he taught the rest of the team the new procedures, and we completed what we needed to by Friday. The best part was that the program went on to be successful and we were small part of it. This teammate let's call him John. John is the kind of person you want to lead and have on your team.

CHAPTER 6

What is the first step?

You know when someone is the leader, when they are the first to help or to offer help. So, how can you help? There is not a greater path, easier path, or more wanted path to leadership, than to problem solve. There are always problems that need solving, including problems with production, problems with customers, problems with personnel, problems with children, aunts, uncles, etc.. There are problems with vendors, suppliers or equipment. When you are look around you, now you can see problems that are there and ones you can solve.

Leaders can solve problems. When you have shown the ability to solve problems, people will bring you more problems. It is reminiscent of the days gone by, when there were kings that ruled their land. Almost every country had a king or queen, who the people would bring them problems to solve. It is kind of a romantic way to think about it. But before you anoint yourself as royalty, consider what I said earlier. You are a servant to your people, who rely on you for leadership.

I look at this relationship as you are at the bottom and you serve everyone else in the organization. That is depicted in the graphic below. Do see where you are? You are there with your long-haired shoe brush.

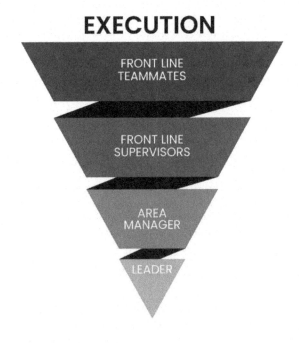

EXECUTION

FRONT LINE
TEAMMATES

FRONT LINE
SUPERVISORS

AREA
MANAGER

LEADER

What problem can you solve? That depends on where you are in the organization. What is the immediate problem in your immediate area? This may be the one thing that aggravates everyone or seems to be the obstacle or the challenge that does not seem to be overcome. Take this problem or challenge, evaluate it, to see how you would solve it and then act. If you have to get support from your co-workers or teammates to get the help be sure talk about the benefit and how life will be better once your solution is implemented. If you can take action right now, then do it. If not then present your solution to the person in charge of the area, with support from your teammates to gain approval then implement. This will do two things for you; 1.) it will show your teammates that you are thinking about things and want to improve them and 2.) it will show the person in charge that you have some ability to problem solve.

When I was in the US Navy, I had several years of experience, but we were experiencing a technology revolution. Much in the same way the world was, computers were changing the way we did things. My role was in communications, which meant we were responsible for messages that came to our ship. These messages carried information for doing business; everything from ammunition, food, fuel, promotions, schedule, and orders among many other things. Think what a small city would need and that is what these messages contained, along with the business of defending a nation. These were important thus keeping track of them and having a historical library of them is important as well. Before computers, this was all done via paper. So, keeping them filed as you would think of in a file cabinet was no longer efficient or desirable. We were now keeping them in the computer. If you have experienced a crashed computer or computer program, you know it can be devastating.

As computers were new, we suffered two or three times, when we lost our library in the computer. Sometimes it hit us hard and others we got by okay.

I decided to devise a plan to export the message library to an external source, so when the main computer crashed, we would have the messages stored as backup. It took some thinking. It took some research and diving into the computer program software to learn more about it. It took some developing of some procedures, steps, and some training, but eventually we had a system. The next crash of the computer system, we were ready. We were able to continue to provide to the rest of the ship their information and we could perform one of the main contributions to our ship's success – deliver messages.

During the time of developing this system, I asked my teammates what they thought would work, wouldn't add to their workload, and would not be too hard to learn. I asked our supervisor what his thoughts were and if he like to contribute to the process. I developed the steps, I tested the steps, I asked one of my teammates to do the steps and when all this was a success; I implemented the new process fully and completely for all.

I solved the problem.

From this time forward, my teammates saw me as the problem solver. They began to bring me more problems to solve. This allowed me to improve position as a leader. A key point here is that when I say position it was the result of work and actions that I took. It was the result of someone appointing me to a position. That's the key difference. I earned it. It is like earning respect. That is when you know you are a true leader, or everyone listens to you because you hold their paycheck.

This got their attention and got them to listen when I spoke. I would hope they thought, maybe this guy has something to say. Whatever the reason they did listen, it was nice have their respect and attention.

When you lead it is a relationship. Having respect allows you to make deeper connections with the people you lead. This allows you to cast your vision. It is a vision for success, how to achieve the next goal, or to make things work better. In this vision, you must include how life will be when the vision is fulfilled, how their life will be better, and what is their role to help make the vision a reality. What people want to know is how can I be successful, while I am helping us be successful? Am I valuable to the cause? Will I make a difference? I believe with a high degree of certainty that people want to know they are useful, serve a purpose and make a difference. I think this makes them feel fulfilled and self-actualized, as though this vision happened because of them. This is because it will. People want to be a part of something bigger than themselves and contribute. You can provide that for them, by casting a vision that includes them. This is a great way to gain followers and teammates; by letting them know how important they are to the cause and to you.

Once you start to lead, you want to make sure you keep leading. The pitfalls of losing the role of leadership most often pertain to character. There are many examples of this throughout history and today. One of the greatest leaders of all time, King David of Israel, lost his position to his son. If you know the story of David, he came on the scene when he slayed the giant with a sling shot. He won many battles in the ancient Middle East and became King. He brought Israel to prominence as the strongest nation in the region. Until, and I am paraphrasing, he stopped doing what brought him to the throne. He stopped engaging with his people, he stopped solving problems, and he stopped leading his army in battle. In short, he rested on his laurels, kept to his inner circle and allowed his son to gain power, through which he stopped doing.

Eventually his son became so powerful that David fled his kingdom for fear of his son.

Remember that what you did yesterday, which may have brought you fame, does not serve today. You have to keep solving problems.

Have you ever looked in a mirror? The person who was looking back at you, is the only person who can help you with the next thing you must possess to lead. That is integrity. Just so we are on the same page – integrity is firm adherence to a code of values. I like the word "firm" in this definition. Because it sets my mind to the position that I need to ensure integrity in my leadership. Integrity in leadership means that I will lead my team in a way that serves them, serves the purpose of them, and never only serves me. If you lead in a way that serves you; in order to get a promotion, make yourself look good, or obtain riches. Integrity in leadership also means that I will be truthful with my teammates, coworkers, and customers. It also applies to my family and community.

Integrity in action looks like this – when you are driving through an empty parking lot, you stop at the stop sign, instead of blowing through it because no one is around. I know, it is a very simple example. But it is one you can easily understand and easily apply to any situation. Do the right thing, even when no one is looking.

You may be skeptical. You may get away with not living with integrity for a time. It may be for a long time, but it will catch up with you. And you will not be able to choose when it does. It will catch up to you at the worst possible time and there is not much you can do to mitigate the effect. The act has been committed, it is in the past and the past cannot be changed. At this point, you do not have much control over what will happen.

I fell on the wrong side of this principle. I had been in the Navy for about four years. I had achieved the paygrade of E-5 which at that time was faster than most. I was on duty that day, which consisted of me processing these messages manually via paper. This was 1988. It was a Saturday morning, early as we had to process messages and have them ready for the crew by 6:45 or 7:00 AM. These messages would be of differing levels of classifications in regard to national security, levels one, two, and three. If you got one of level two or three classification that required "more processing". I would be off duty when this was done and head out to see my girlfriend who was hours away. More processing was not on my mind.

Of course, I got one of the high classification messages. I read it and did not say much. I also knew that it would take time to process and I also knew that we could request another copy if this one somehow got lost. I decided to put this copy in a bag for destruction. No harm, no foul right? Wrong! What transpired was a series of lies I chose to tell to cover my tracks. And each lie, I got deeper and deeper in trouble. The end result was that at the order of the command one of my teammates found the message which they knew I had to have put there, since it came in on my day of duty. I finally confessed too many days and too many lies too late. I was not court martialed but received punishment none the less. I missed seeing my girlfriend for the next 45 days and my parents' 50th wedding anniversary surprise party. This was high price to pay for a few minutes of time. No matter how many times I thought I could outsmart the system and the people, I could not control what happened. Someone more determined than I and who was on the side of the truth defeated me. I lost my integrity. When you do that, the best course is to own up to it right away, make things right, and begin again to build it back up.

What I was trying to do was manipulation and that is selfish. That is not leadership. I was trying to make it about me and what I wanted. That will always backfire, and it did on me. Sooner or later, it will for you too. Leadership must be about what the organization wants, the people need, and what you should do for both.

When you get your perspective fixated on that, your actions, your words, and your results will begin to show how well your leadership is progressing.

CHAPTER 7

You are Leading – Let's go!

The project was off the ground and we had some success. There were people from other teams from other companies that were supporting other parts of the network asking to come on our team! I was very proud, pleased, and relieved.

That is a great commentary of people's behavior, when something is going well, you will have bandwagon jumpers. This happens a lot in sports when a team is doing well. All of a sudden, their fans seem to multiply by the thousands.

I asked myself, how can I get this team to go even higher?

Earlier I shared with you an experience leading a team of 10 individuals to support a cybersecurity project. The team was able to start their day and be productive. However, I knew that there would be challenges that would come up. Unforeseen challenges, how can we be prepared for them?

I decided to start to challenge them. Even though they were meeting the requirements of the job, I wanted them to be top-notch. Every business has competition. The market is built on competition. Ford competes with Chevy, Microsoft with Apple, and Levi's with Lee. I wanted to do the job well but also to impress the customer enough to give us more work and scare the competition away.

Out of the 10 people on the team, I had two people that worked in the office with me, who were the developers of technical policy that was implemented for the network; e.g. they configured how the network would behave and what each user could do or not do. Each of them did a piece of the configuration and one did the testing. I pushed them to find ways of making it quicker, faster, and more effective. I challenged the tester that when he went out in the field to make sure the technical change performed properly; to make a personal connection with the customer he would see that day. I wanted him to make sure they knew they were here to help, answer questions, make the customer be at ease with what was going on, and that they could reach out to us at any point to help or if they had questions. I asked him to be sincere, when he delivered this message. This creates an atmosphere of appreciation to the client and a feeling that we care about them and their work, which of course was true.

The developer in the office with me, I additionally challenged him to guide and train the tester to one day take his place as the lead policy developer. This cannot be overemphasized when leading your team, each person must feel that you have the next step for them in their career, something to strive for. The developer had the next step too. I talked to him about teaching his teammate did not mean I was replacing him but helping him prepare for his next step. This relieves the pressure for him and allowed him to do the training effectively.

An additional benefit to having your teammates train and teach their replacements is a rule that I think stands up well. The rule is that when you must teach a subject by the act of teaching, it helps the trainer understand it that much better. It deepens their knowledge and confidence in the subject. This is supported by questions they may get from the people they are teaching. This has an effect of strengthening the trainer in their subject matter, when people feel they know and do their jobs well they perform better, are more fulfilled, and more committed. They are also easier to lead.

I asked the members of the team that went out in the field to assess, test, and configure the various network computer servers to think about how they could do the job better. At the beginning of the project, we had developed processes and procedures to complete the job. But what often happens is the plan cannot account for everything that occurs, as "the best-laid schemes of mice and men are sure to go awry".[3] I challenged them to think about "what could we do to make it go faster, less intrusive for the client, and safer for the server". Again, I challenged them to make a personal connection with each client we came in contact with. This would begin the development of these team members as leaders and leave the client with the impression that we truly cared about them or at a minimum saw them as people. In short, provide good customer service, a la Chick Fil A.

Up to this point, there is one especially important point left out. The leader can ask all they want but if they do not provide the example then the ask will fall on deaf ears. The leader has to challenge himself. Look at it this way, for every ask made you have to ask yourself at least an equal value ask or more. You have to become the mirror for the team to guide themselves.

---

[3] Robert Burns, "To a Mouse" 1786

I decided to do these things

- Be sure to be on time for everything

- At each encounter with a client or teammate have a conversation

- Communicate about everything

- Perform at the highest level I could

- Be consistent

- Take responsibility for goals

As we stood on the corner of a busy street in a major US city, we waited, again for Jim to arrive at our meeting location, so we could leave for work. We were carpooling to the job. This is very annoying when 3 to 5 people are waiting for one person. Being on time shows respect for the people you are meeting and that you care about their time. It also says that you can manage and lead yourself well. If you subscribe to the philosophy that fundamentals will lead you to success, then being on time is a fundamental that needs to be hit every time. When you are late it wastes money, time is money. When you are late it weakens your position, especially when you are trying to influence someone to buy from you or agree with your position. It also will make you seem scatterbrained or emotionally unfocused. You may apologize through your nose when you are late, but the damage is already done.

There are no good excuses for being late. Where you are and when is under your control. You must admit that it is your fault when you are late. Traffic and sleeping in are not reasons for being late. Being on time takes some planning, adjustment, and commitment. It can be controlled. It communicates to the other party that you are organized, in control, and professional.

The leader's job is the people. As you pull into your parking spot arriving at work after navigating traffic, you have spilled your coffee, and you just want to get to your desk to get started. On your way to your desk, you pass by several people, but you do not talk to them because you have many things to do today. You want to get them done.

You just walked past the most important part of your day. The people you passed. The opportunity to connect with them is valuable. Each time you pass someone in the hall, at the water cooler, or in the restroom is an opportunity. For them, it says so much about you when you recognize and interact with them as people. This builds trust with them and allows for the relationship to flourish. Engaging with your people, to converse about the business, the game, or their interests show them you value them.

No matter how big or small the task of the moment is, communicate about it entirely. Your team needs to hear from you 'what is going on'. They will appreciate being in the loop. They will trust you as the leader and the director of the project, company, or family. This transparency makes them feel comfortable that they are not missing something. Communicating is not a one and done event. As long as necessary, talk about the details while the project is going until it completes. Things do change and events happen. This causes people to think, 'how does this change things?'. By continuing to communicate, it will answer the questions and allow your team to focus on their role.

Further communicate and repeat the vision of the team, project, or organization. While you do this, assess whether people are onboard with it. If not, find a way to get them on the same page, unify, and contribute. All people are different, some will come on board quickly, while others will need more time to accept and others will need more data and evidence. But they will come, your job is to continue to garner support and gain their buy-in.

While I was challenging my teammates to be better, I just walked away satisfied they would and went to play golf. No, I did not. It would be nice though. I looked at myself to see where I could improve. I made sure to continue to support each team member daily, to complete my tasks as quickly and accurately as I could and follow up with the customer often. I wanted them to understand I was engaged with the project and it was important to me.

I studied the subject matter to remain familiar with the latest technology, kept measurable status on progress, and answered questions efficiently. I also looked for ways to provide above and beyond service to the client. Although we were hired to provide technical service, I observed the way the client was operating their network. I observed their policies to analyze whether I could find ways to improve how they did business. I did this for several areas of their operations. They did not specifically ask for this, but I provided it none the less. You need to be careful with this. Do not provide something for your customer before you have delivered what they have originally asked. Therefore, you must be sure they are satisfied with the delivery of services or products first. You must have good communication with them to ask directly or gauge their willingness to accept this "extra work". When you can deliver more value than expected or pay for you have a happy client and develop a reputation for being a valuable vendor.

Trust plays a big part in your team coming along and staying along with you. One of the best ways to gain trust is to be consistent. Consistency is an undervalued characteristic of good leadership. Consistency says you can be counted on. When you show up over and over the same, with the same attitude, the same methods, the same vision, and the same message, that is consistency. People will begin to rely on that. They know that is one thing they will not have to worry about.

Is there someone in your life like that? Day in and day out, you know what you are getting? What is your opinion of that person? For me, that is a comfort and a reliable source. Someone I know I can go to with a problem, be around, and want to follow.

When you have consistency as a leader, your people will look at you as the backbone of the organization. If you are consistently kind, they know they can talk to you. If you are consistently inspiring, they know they can come to get a jump from you. If you consistently listen, they know they are heard. If you are consistently praising, they know they will be appreciated. When you are consistent, you set up a safe environment.

As I shared in a previous chapter, when you are leading, you no longer are worried about your performance but the team, organization, business's performance. You are responsible for it all working. You have to take personal responsibility for achieving the goals. This may be one of the harder parts of leadership to grasp fully at first. Although others are doing the work, you are holding yourself responsible.

You have to ask; how can I help? You can resource them; you can encourage them, you can do what you can do to contribute, and you can guide to the goal. Keep your eye on the prize; then nudge, push, and prod the team to the goal.

One of the greatest attributes you can display is vulnerability. This return on investment for being vulnerable is enormous. I use vulnerability here is as willingness to be known. Many leaders keep their people, teammates, and family at an arm's length. They may feel that this is best, as leading is a job that requires hard decisions, tough conversations, and unpopular choices. Therefore, they create a moat around them. My guess is this prevents them from being hurt, makes it easier to make the unpopular choice, or have the tough conversation. This is short-sighted. When you allow yourself to be known, you establish a relationship with the person you are leading. When this happens you create companionship, with your team and you. This allows them to see you and you them. This creates space for your team to succeed with you rather than for you. Therefore, when you those hard decisions, tough conversations, or unpopular choices, they know your heart. The result is clarity of communication and importantly, trust.

CHAPTER 8

You have it going – What's next?

We discussed a scenario earlier where 'John' came up with a solution that got our team out of a tricky spot and helped us deliver our project on time. As John was a valuable member of the technical team, this was his strength. This was not his first opportunity to shine as a technical savior. However, I knew that his career would have a ceiling on it as a technician versus becoming a project or program manager. Therefore, I thought, "How can I help his career?" I evaluated what I needed to teach him, what were the skillsets, the topics of business to teach, and how to become a project and program manager. Once I had a game plan, I needed to talk to him.

First, I needed to know if he wanted to hear what my vision was for him. If I did not pass this test, then it would be useless for me to try.

I began the conversation by telling him how well I thought he was doing, giving him examples of what I noticed that he did well. This established that I appreciated his work. I asked him what his plan was for his career. He told me what he was thinking. I also asked him what his life plan, more kids? Bigger house? When did he want to retire, etc. Once I had this information, I realized my plan may fit with his. I began to share what I was thinking for his next steps. I wanted him to know that I was thinking about his career and how I could help him advance, earn more money, and be more secure. I wanted him to become a leader in the organization and be as successful as he wanted to be.

I think this scenario plays out in many companies. The one or two people who seem to get the work done get selected to become leaders. But this is where the problem or the shortcoming comes in; the go getters are often selected to become leaders but without the preparation and training of the skill set of being a leader. You see, technical performance, in this case - or any other skillset: accounting, sales, welding, customer service or any other skill - does not translate into being a leader. The difference I am talking about is between producing and leading. Up to this point, John was a great producer, but I was asking him to become a great leader. I needed to equip him with the skills of being a leader. But first we needed to talk about a mindset shift.

A shift can occur from a performer or producer to a leader. I have seen this happen time and again with organizations that I have worked at, worked for, or customers that I have supported. The shining star gets the promotion, the leadership/management group presumes that he or she will continue to shine in the new position. But over time the person seems to struggle, fails, and the whole organization suffers. There is suffering because they lost a good performer and gained a bad leader. Now, there are two positions that need filling or improved.

Therefore, this mind shift must happen before, during, and after the producer takes on the new role. The mind shift from producer to leader looks like this:

Producer	Leader
Concentrates on tasks	Concentrates on the team
Feels indispensable in what they do	Feels responsible for what others do
Possesses tunnel vision	Possesses team vision
Thinks, "How can I help?"	Thinks, "Who can help us?"
Asks, "What can I do?"	Asks, "What can we do?"
Produces through addition	Produces through multiplication

Put simply, to shift from producer to leader, a person must make the mind shift from me to we.[4]

As I was speaking to John about enhancing his career, I talked to him about this. He would be responsible for more than just him, e.g. performing well to keep his job. He would be expected to help his teammates, me, and the customers/clients. I thought that he would be ecstatic about the possible promotion. But he was a little hesitant. I put his fears to rest by telling him that will not be an overnight change. He would continue to do his current job but over time I would be "training" him on his new responsibilities.

---

[4] Maxwell, John C. Good Leaders Ask Great Questions: Your Foundation for Successful Leadership (Kindle Locations 3217-3233). Center Street. Kindle Edition.

My first step was to work on changing his mindset from me to we. I can remember during our first conversations when he would ask questions or, when I would be explaining why we do this or that, him saying "Oh, I did not think of that", or "I see now". These were good signs that he was getting it and his mind set was shifting.

What I also did was invite him to meetings that he was not usually invited to previously. These included meetings on budget, planning, business development, personnel decisions, and training plans. Before each meeting, I would have a pre-meeting with him to brief on the purpose of the meeting, expectations, our objectives, any questions he had, and, most importantly, that he was welcomed and expected to raise questions or have a contribution to the meeting. I wanted him to know he deserved a seat at the table, he deserved to be a contributor, and that I wanted him to grow.

After each meeting, I would have a quick call or meeting with him to answer any further questions he had and get his perspective on next steps.

But, the other thing that I did was to not assume I was solely responsible for his metamorphosis. I encouraged him and supported his application in the leadership cohort program that our company offered - again, in the effort to arm him with skills and perspectives of a leader versus a producer.

If you're a good producer, you probably know how you personally contribute to the vision of the organization. Ask yourself, "How does this team contribute to the vision?" and "How can every individual member contribute to the team?" Your job is to maximize the team's effort to fulfill the vision. John had the skills and knowledge that each of the other members needed to do the job. I had him set up meetings with every other member of the team to discuss where they were in their projects, so he could share his knowledge with them, offer help, and start see the bigger picture.

As this process progressed, our conversations began to change from me asking him how he is doing to how is so and so doing. I must admit this was quite enjoyable to hear similar reactions and statements about our teammates that I experienced. It's fun to have someone walk in your shoes. He would say things like "I told him to watch out for that or do this, and he didn't do it" and "We got it done and to the customer on time even though we had this challenge." When I heard these things, I knew he was in the right path and gaining experience.

This also told me his perspective was moving from 'what do I have to do' to 'what do we have to do?' This is the biggest shift for a superlative producer to transform into a leader. Often their productiveness comes from their ability to focus, which a leader needs also but in a broader perspective. This can be difficult for some folks to get used to. I understand. It may feel like you are losing control or not focusing on your tasking. But trust me, this is where you need to move your perspective to what the team needs to do to help it succeed.

Asking for help is often the hardest thing for a person to do. It is almost like admitting defeat, in some ways it is but this is where our weaknesses show up. We all have weaknesses and it is important to identify them, accept them, then ask for help in your area of weakness. Therefore, the DISC Assessment is so valuable because it identifies what our weaknesses are. As the leader, many times you have to assess and be realistic about your team's limits then ask for help. I know this is admitting a vulnerable spot to an outside source, and that may be scary, risky, and difficult. But you want your team to win, don't you? Then we must ask for help, whether that is training, advice, or outsourcing. The goal is to succeed. A good way to look at this is when you reach for this help you add another person to the celebratory party when you succeed, adding another entity to the success.

Inevitably, there will be challenges, changes, corrections, and opportunities along the way from time to time. At this point, a new leader must think 'what can we do'. As a producer, one only has to think about 'what do I have to do?' This includes work harder, learn a new skill, or adjust my schedule. But as a leader you have to think about all the pieces of the organization. What does the front desk person have to do, shipping, manufacturing, service desk, sales team etc. It is a much bigger task to consider the answer to all those questions. And this may answer the question you had of your current leader; "what does he do all day long anyways?"

John was the hardest worker on the team. I wanted to capitalize on this commitment. When he worked harder, he was adding by addition. Each hour in a day he worked he added to the team by 1. What I wanted him to do was add by 2 or 3 or 4. It wasn't that the team was not producing under my leadership but I wanted them to respond to him as well, to see him, for now, as my number 2. This would pay dividends later. If he can inspire them to work as he did, by his example and leadership, then he was on his way and so were we. Therefore, his work would actually multiply the production of the team because he would be pulling and encouraging the team along with him. This is multiplication.

Why is multiplication important? Once the team is responding to John then, as new people are added to the team, I can take them under my wing to get them up to speed while John continues to lead the original team developed by me and now led by him. Yes, the team will morph a bit, taking on characteristics of John. That will be fine as I have vetted him, in a sense, through observation, performance, and teaching. I know he has the goods to lead and do at least 80% as well as me. The reality was that he often did better.

As John was developing his skills, I was hearing more and more from him about the personal things he was learning about other teammates. I was also getting the right questions from him. He would ask about how to handle this or that challenge with a project or person. I would teach how he had to connect with the person, to begin to trust them and how he could set them up for success. I told him how he must equip them to succeed with whatever they may be lacking which may be process skills, technical skills or self-confidence.

This did not happen overnight, the transformation to a leader. There are a few opportunities each day to lead, then you have to get the work done. So, it took some time, but it was worth it. John developed into a good leader, the team responded and accepted him as a leader. There were some missteps and areas where he did not do the best, but that is to be expected. This is a first-time situation, not many of us do well the first time. Do you remember riding a bike? My first time was not a great show either but eventually I got the bike under control and was riding smoothly.

You can make this transition. Your first step is to want it. The second and third steps come much easier after that. Some of you will feel as though you are losing control. You were doing your job just fine and everything was in order, things were getting done and all was neat and tidy. But now, the world just got bigger and there are more moving pieces. What am I going to do with all these teammates, customers, and processes? There might even be lions, tigers, and bears! Okay, probably not, but it did make you laugh, didn't it? I always say you have to be having fun at what you do or why do it?

It reminds me of when I ascended to a position of training lead, while I was in the Navy. I had to make sure everyone in our division was trained in their position, would be ready to participate in promotion exams, and be successful. This included developing the training plans, reporting status, delivering the training, and making sure my teammates absorbed the information. In the military, we had the extra incentive to train well because at some point, it could mean life or death. I have to be honest, when I first learned I was going to be training, I thought "what are they thinking giving this to me?" But what choice did I have? I dove in and the water was wet. I learned the program requirements, what I needed to do and how to do it. My leaders support my learning so I could succeed. But I thought, "How I can I make this better?" I remembered a conversation I had earlier in my career at a previous duty station. A senior member of the Navy had told me that he created small tests for each task within our career field. I liked this idea, since it could give me feedback on how well the training program was being assimilated by the team. I created the first test for the most basic task we had to do. Remember this was 1987. There were no computers on ships back then. I had to type this out on an IBM Select III typewriter. For those of you much younger than I, this was a mechanical device that is like today's computer printers but with the keyboard attached and a striking device to imprint the letter on a piece of paper. It was time consuming and slow to create this test on paper. Once completed, I made copies to deliver the test to the team. The day came to deliver the test and it was a success. The team liked the idea of knowing exactly what they need to know and do, I knew if they were receiving the training and applying it, and leadership had a barometer to know how well each person was doing.

I did not have to do this. A test was not a requirement to properly do the job. But it served the team to do this, the whole team. I could have done the minimum, or a little above the minimum, and would have been fine. The job would have been done. But once I turned my focus away from me to we, then something much bigger happened and we all benefited. Looking back, it was not that much more to do, but it was more. And more is what you will do when you become a leader, and everyone will benefit.

CHAPTER **9**

Grow Other Leaders

I mention John in previous chapters. John as the one you want on your team, John is the one who I picked to become a leader, a leader I would lead. John came to me as a young man. I think he was less than 30 years old. We had forged a relationship through third parties, having worked together in a process where we represented different clients, and through some personal time while attending a national conference in his hometown. My assessment of him was that he was a solid guy.

Our relationship allowed each of us to share from our personal life. We crossed the boundary from professional to personal. John recently had his first child and he lives in Charleston, South Carolina. His parents, and those of his wife, live in northern Georgia, near Atlanta. John and his wife were very proud of their newborn son. They visited home as often as they could on the weekends as both he and his wife worked full time. He shared with me the visits home and said the words that changed his life, "It is hard to leave my folks house, my mom cries and she kisses my boy good-bye at the end of the weekend." He continued, "My wife and I cry as we leave our parents. It is very hard. We want our son to grow up knowing their grandparents and want our parents to have time with him." You see, although John and I worked for the same company, he did not work for me. My heart was filled with compassion for John. I could see his dream scenario and wanted his life to be as he saw it best. I asked myself what I could do.

As I look back now, I can see that using the concepts, techniques, and methods I talk about in this book allowed me to build a business line in this entrepreneurial company, which I had cognizance over. Simply put, I could hire and fire, make budget decisions and do what I felt best to serve my clients inside the overall company. I had grown and established myself well enough to be trusted with this.

Yes, I was going to hire John. A good number of people on my team at the time worked remotely from the clients. Therefore, it didn't matter where John lived, as long as he was willing to travel from time to time to the client site.

I took action. I went to my immediate boss, again I apologize, to ask about the "politics" of hiring John away from another division. He gave me guidance. I called John's supervisor to share with him John's story and my plan. He could see the merit of the plan; John may be lost to the company soon, as his heart strings were being pulled. Therefore, it was beneficial to keep John in the company rather than lose him. His supervisor agreed, reluctantly, but he agreed. I was set.

I offered my plan to John, I asked him if he wanted to move home to be near his parents, his son's grandparents, and work remotely. I asked him if he would be willing to leave his current job to come work for me? He was astonished, a bit overwhelmed; almost not believing this could happen to him. I assured him that I spoke with his boss's boss already and that all was okay with him. John was a loyal guy. John said he had to talk with his wife to make the decision, but he came back to me the next day with the "yes" for which I was looking. And off we went.

I could not have done this for John, if I had not been a servant leader. If I had not been a leader, I would not have a business line or the autonomy to make this offer. I would not have had the success to serve as the basis to allow a man, his wife, and young son the confidence to believe making a major life change would work out. Further, if I had not valued relationships and people, I would have never been presented with the opportunity to serve John and his family. He never would have shared this personal story about what was weighing on his heart and mind. My ability as a servant leader was the fruit of labor, growing, reflection, and willingness to try new things. More on that later.

John once wrote me about his experience with me as his leader and being on the team. He shared this:

"So, kinda like I was saying the other day, what you were to me as a boss was very different from any other employer to employee relationship. I think one of the big factors for this was because we were peers/counterparts before you became my boss at [our company]. We spent a good deal of time on the phone while you were at the [decision authority's] office and I was supporting [the technical authority's office]. So, from our respective positions, we had already developed a great working relationship and we were interfacing on a personal level as well. I was about to become a dad for the first time and you were sharing your experiences in that area well before you were in the boss position above me. So I think all that played a role into our future working relationship. Once you were in the that supervisor position over me, you seemed to always work with me from that personal connection perspective. More as a mentor than a

supervisor. I think that's the big difference from other bosses/supervisors I worked with before and since."

(The [] brackets added to not identify our clients.)

John believing in me was the first step, as I said before. But that did not guarantee his success or ours. How do I get John to start to act like, and become, a leader? To continue from the last chapter, the key tool/technique to finish the job was to use delegation. Delegation is the leader's best friend. It allows the leader to provide opportunities for teammates to grow.

What does a leader provide in delegation? The leader provides those jobs and tasks that he knows he can allow others to do that they will do at least 80% as well as he can. He must pick those jobs that he knows someone else can do, not one that only he can do. This decision will take some thought and reflection. You have to ask, "What should I do that no one else can do or should do?" This may be something that only you are qualified to do, that makes the decision easy. But what if that is not the case? How else would you decide? A couple of examples come to mind. The first is from a local company that I recently conducted a DISC workshop for. They hired me to present them with some DISC assessments for senior leadership, then a workshop to explain DISC to them. The CEO was a man we'll call 'Larry', so I researched Larry through his social media platforms to learn what I could about him and the company. There were five people on the senior leadership team and I researched all of them. What I found was interesting. One of the leaders, in sales, 'Archie', was actually the founder of the company, but not the CEO. This was interesting because, by my thinking, wouldn't the founder want to be, or rightfully be, the CEO? But this was not the case, he had delegated that position to Larry. Why? One reason is that Archie held the passion and vision and ability to communicate the purpose of the company to new and current clients. Larry had the ability to lead the company from the front to make the decisions necessary as the CEO. Archie saw the skills of Larry and evaluated his own, then made the decision of delegation, which was best for the company.

This arrangement is working. From the workshop I found a leadership team that worked well together, were committed to each other, and were growing themselves through their leadership training program, which I was able to be a part of. Coincidently, their DISC profiles said that Larry would be best as CEO and Archie as Sales, it confirmed they got it right.

Once you know what you can and cannot delegate, and who you can delegate to, then you are ready to delegate.

Why? Anytime I ask a teammate to complete a task for me I always like to include the why behind it. It gives context to the task and allows the person doing to task to fully immerse themselves in it, be creative, and have their eyes wide open. Delegating is the tool a leader uses to make himself most productive, successful, and effective. But it is also is the tool that serves the most important point of leadership, to create more leaders. When you use delegation you:

- Involve others, not just direct them

- Reward good work

- Create an atmosphere of growth

- Build further trust and intimacy

- Create another leader

- Add productivity to your organization

- Add new ideas and talent at the top

Another advantage to delegation is it covers the gaps in the leader's knowledge, insight, and blind spots. There is not a person on earth that knows everything, can do everything, or can see everything. You, as the leader, need people around you that can support the 360-degree view of the situation. They can produce or fix things that you cannot. Remember how John saved our butts on the navigation system? They can see a problem before it blind sides you and have talents in areas that you do not. They make the team stronger, more productive, and successful.

So how do you do this delegation anyway, after you decide what to delegate and to who?

Here is a guide:

Start small. You have a teammate that is ready for the next level of their career. This is a key and pivotal point in your relationship with them. You must tread lightly, as the saying goes. You do not want to overwhelm them which could slow their progress down or injure the relationship. What you can start with is a fact-finding mission. Whatever the project or task may be, have them research about it, ask questions of teammates, or even see what competitors may be doing. In this way you are having them educate themselves about it to raise their expertise. Then have them report back to you what they find. During this time, they will find any issues with the project that need to be overcome and possible objections to proceeding with the project. They can also identify issues with implementation, resources, time, or objections from the team, the market, or financing. These are all things to know before beginning the planning of project or implementation of something known or newly developed.

At this point, ask them what they think. This is very empowering to your teammate. There is no greater respect and consideration than being asked, and then listened to, about what your recommendation will be. Ask questions about the recommendation to dig deeper into their thoughts or to encourage them to think deeper. Get to know their vision by asking this powerful question, "What does X look like when Y happens?" This allows them to paint the picture for you, to be fully immersed in their solution and to own it. I love to gently challenge them here. Be careful though, I want to challenge them so they can defend their strategy. The idea here is that if they can defend it or explain the rationale for the success, to get to the objective - then it is comprehensive. They have thought it through. You are collaborating with them; you have raised them from teammate to colleague and invited them to the table.

Once you feel comfortable and confident that they have the full picture, it is time for action. Give them your approval to move forward. You want them to succeed, therefore do not give them the go signal, until you are certain they will succeed. This is their first big project and can be a defining moment in their career. This is the time for encouragement, the baby bird is moving from the nest for the first time. You may want to point out where the hawks like to roam, or the foxes, or the wildcats. Encourage them about the plan, what you liked about it and how you thought it would work. If you found something that you particularly liked, be sure to mention it. And more than once, they may be insecure about their first steps, so encourage them often.

What you must be sure not to do, is act on the temptation to take over to ensure victory. Remember, they are spreading their wings. You gave them the green light. You are in a support role here. This is their time to grow, learn, and thrive. This is the making of a leader, someone who can independently maneuver in your team and business. It may be hard to sit on your hands, but you must, in order to allow space for them.

They are on their way now. They may have some wins and the project is moving. Allow them to act on their own. They do not have get permission with each step. But you are still guiding them, they are still playing with a net, and the net is you. They maintain the net, by having them report results back to you. This is how you can keep an "eye" on things. You must, of course, still have responsibility and accountability. But you can also perform damage control if something goes wrong, which it inevitably will. You know by now that nothing in life is perfect and, since this is their first time, something may go wrong. But just as you put them in charge of the project, you also put them in charge of fixing what is going wrong.

Again, ask them what they plan to do, offer your expertise where it is necessary. You should always be teaching, not telling or directing. This is key, if you begin to direct, you push them back into their role of being another teammate, rather than one of the leaders. This takes some practice. Our tendencies may be to fix it immediately, or become anxious about the problem and want to solve it. This, again, will have a detrimental effect on the new leader. This may signal you have lost faith. Obviously, this you do not want to happen. This is a great teaching point; leaders solve problems, and this is how a leader is established the quickest. This fact didn't change from making yourself a leader, as we discussed in an earlier chapter. Allow them to solve the problem. This is where they can make their mark. The story will be told of them and the project - 'even though we had this problem, we saw the project through and were successful'. Who does not like that ending? There is merit and perseverance in that story that builds teams, cohesion, and character around the new leader. Your team has gotten stronger and bigger! And a new leader is born.

The final step, that you have been working towards, is to give them full authority to do the job. Full authority means you have fully given them the reins, you have handed the baby over to them, and they now own the process. There is a story that has floated around my circles that illustrates this pretty well. There are two executives who were coming out of their building on their way to lunch. They come across the man who was tending to the greenery around the building. As usual, they stop to say hello and chat a minute. As they were chatting, they both notice that the rake the man was using did not have but one or two teeth in it. This, obviously, makes his job tougher to do. They ask him why he is using the rake. He tells them this is the one he has to use. They ask him why he has not gone out to buy another rake and find he does not have permission or "authority" to purchase another rake. This was illuminating and alarming to the executives. They assured the man that this problem would be solved immediately. They corrected the lack of authority for this man to be able to have the authority to do the job correctly and with the proper tools. Additionally, they looked throughout the company to see where else authority needed to be given to ensure execution was timely and efficient.

You want your new leader to have the responsibility, accountability, and authority to fulfill the role for which you have developed them. To do it any other way, is to make them fly with only one wing. They will always have to land back at your desk to finish the flight. This will create a bottleneck at best, but a growth obstacle at worst. Let them fly!

CHAPTER 10

They Grow You

There once was a young, loud-mouthed, cocky kid who had all the answers and he knew it. If you have ever been in the room with Mike, you knew he was there. You could hear him above all other folks in the room, and that's if he wasn't in your face loudly telling you what was on his mind. He had no trouble expressing his opinions and thoughts. In meeting him, you had to brace yourself for the onslaught of conversation you were going to engage in, voluntarily or not, but also laugh to yourself about the exuberant persona coming at you. It was almost cartoonish. But that is Mike. You could not help but like him or keep yourself from being engaged with him. He was magnetic.

When I met Mike, it was part of a training mission on one of the US Navy's Fast Frigate Fleets in Norfolk, VA in 1997. I was on his ship to train him and his teammates. Although I outranked Mike by four paygrades, he had no problem interrupting my training to tell me I was not exactly right, at least as he saw it. Or not how "they did it here." I bet you are not surprised by this.

At that moment, I thanked him for his input but asked him to hold on to the end of the training and I would be glad to answer any more of his questions, of which I assured him my training would answer most. Just sit tight Mike, I told him. After training, we conversed about the topics and came to an agreement that we were both right, depending. As I would find out throughout our relationship, this was a big victory. He was a determined man.

Our relationship continued through the rest of my 20-year career, which ended in 2004, and he was one of the "side boys" for my retirement ceremony. Side boys create an alley; they stand on each side of the walkway, to and from the stage, for the distinguished guests to walk through.

Over the years, we played many rounds of golf in our off-time, sharing the tales of life, the Navy, and God's Country, his beloved Colorado. He told me how John Elway is the greatest living human on the planet and how he would beat me on the next hole. I remember one round when we finished and he asked me what my score was, "75" I said.

"No way!" he said.

"Haven't you been paying attention?" I replied.

"I cannot let it end like that, let's go to the putting green and see if I can beat you there." My objections were no match for him, so off we went to the putting green to continue to compete so he could win. I told you he was determined.

After my retirement ceremony was complete, I gave my final remarks. During my remarks, I captured the essence of my career; what the Navy had meant to me. Each person from my family who came to celebrate, I addressed individually on what they meant to me. I did the same for my current and former teammates in attendance. I told the story of how I decided to join the Navy, how it turned out, and gave counsel to the young sailors in the audience on how much it was worth it to serve for 20 years, how fast it goes, and to please follow my footsteps. I told stories of lost shipmates, who I miss every day and how they impacted my life.

Mike pulled me aside so we could talk in private and, as usual, he talked. "Now, do not tell anyone what I am about to say, but your speech touched me, you showed your heart, class, and that you truly cared about what you were doing. I was listening to the other sailors talk to each during your speech and you affected them too. Thank you for your guidance on my career. I am proud to know you. And, again, do not tell anyone I told you that." He laughed and so did I. My allergies must have been bothering me that day, as they made my eyes water.

Mike and I remained in touch throughout the years and still do today. I went to his commissioning as an officer some years later. He has had quite a career.

Our relationship picks up right where we left off, whether it was two weeks ago we last spoke, two months, or two years. After five or 10 minutes, it's as if there was no time wasted. Do you have friends like that? Colleagues? Mentors?

I am sure you do. These are the people that create the fabric of your life. They push you to be better, think bigger, and become more. When you invest in them, they also invest in you. When you grow them, they grow you. There was not a day in Mike's life where he doubted anything about himself, and that rubs off on people, like it did on me. By investing what I knew, it allowed space for his gifts to be invested in me.

You have invested in your team at this point, delegated some duties to them, created a new leader, or even a new department/division/business around them. Their skills and success push you further and further in your growth. They may, and probably will, surpass you. Mike sure did.

He pushed me to continue to achieve more in a corporate career. Many of my colleagues did. There were John, Sarah, Chauncey, Doug, Carrie, Candace, Lawrence, Nancy, Maria, Dave, Larry, and Andy who pushed me to learn more, do more, and achieve more. For some it was because I wanted to show them it could be done, for some because I did not want to disappoint them, and for others because they depended on me, and themselves, for a paycheck.

I had to learn more because now I was running the business line. The requirements were broad-ranging; contracts, execution, technical, finances, leadership, customer relations, and business development. My position required me to know, in-depth, each of the tasks necessary to progress the business but also, more importantly, sustain it.

This was not entirely up to me. Do not get me wrong, we had a team. However, to achieve superlative results, which I demanded of myself and my team, I had to master these subjects to make sure they were executed correctly. This would lead us to success.

Once I had these mastered, I would teach these to the team, or work closely with them to provide input and leadership. I spoke earlier about how I worked with John.

But he was not the only one. Each of my team members had many talents, and I like to think I encouraged them along the way. Sarah, for example, came to my team with some good technical skills in cybersecurity, but needed work on the process of compliance. She was a real go-getter and learned quickly, moving up in knowledge and responsibility. She was hard to keep in her seat. She soon merited a raise and a promotion. She worked on her program, then became the assistant security manager for a developing program that modernized all of the networks for every ship and submarine in the Navy. She pushed me to keep up with her ambition, although she outdistanced me in many ways. She moved to a government position for a while, then back to the private industry, always seeking the next challenge. I was happy recently to help her move into a new position that enhanced her career and fit her family life. She is in a good place. Her qualifications and experience today were part of the plan I had for her and she is one of the most qualified individuals in her field. I am proud to say I gave her a start, solely based on her good attitude and enthusiasm. She worked hard to become what she is today, and I did what I could to help her on her path. I am sure her career is far from over.

I say that because, during our time together, I nominated her to be a part of the cohort leadership program, to which she was accepted, and arranged for her to be mentored by one of the top female executives in our company. I have no doubt this is still paying dividends, as this mentor later became a secretary of armed service. More on that later.

Sarah taught me not to be afraid to go after what you wanted. I cannot exactly tell you what motivated her; a desire to excel, financial security, status, or plain competition. But I will tell you this, if something did not sit right with her, or she saw an opportunity, she did not let the grass grow under feet. She was moving. I guess you can say she was an action person, she knew results came from action. Success and obtainment were not far behind. She was the 'go for it' kind of gal. And she succeeded.

Laurence was the most authoritatively versed cybersecurity professional I ever met. He could tell you why you were doing something, what the law, regulation, or directive was that referenced what we were doing. He also had a great ability to keep the big picture in focus constantly. He never lost sight of the objective.

I could go on and on covering the talents, strengths, and accomplishments of all my teammates, but I want to tell you more about what they gave back to me. What they gave back was triple what I gave them. You see, when you give, it kickstarts the receiving process. It is why being unselfish has just rewards. As a leader, you can be a taker or a giver. As a teammate, you can be a taker or a giver. When you are a leader that gives, and you find teammates that give, then you have got something special.

What my teammates gave back to me is very precious. These are internal things that paid big dividends then, and still do now. One of which is devotion. They were devoted to me, to what I was trying to accomplish, and who we were. This showed on two occasions with one team member, when another company tried to recruit her with money and an internal competitor tried to recruit her to another division. She came to me both times, not to ask for more but to say, "they tried to take me but I told them I work with you and I am good where I am". That type of devotion is not common today when people move from job to job to seek greener pastures and opportunities. This also tells me that people see a future of growth and opportunity for which they want to stay. In reality, I think it is also the culture. They felt as though they were part of something bigger than just themselves. We had a way about us that separated us from the pack, not that we were better, but different. In a kind of a way, a family. I appreciate their devotion. I never took it for granted and knew that I had to keep cultivating it. What I did to earn it yesterday would not attract tomorrow's. I had to keep working.

My team would also be the ultimate backup device. As I said earlier, I had to wear many hats, and sometimes my schedule would get overloaded with meetings, tasks, or customer calls. I would not always have enough time in the day, or I would get tired. There were days when they would pick up my slack to help carry the load. It benefitted them too, so the team would continue to move forward. I would not be too prideful not to allow them to help me. Having developed them for different areas of the business this made them, me, and the business flexible to handle the shifting demands on it. I know we would all like our days to follow exactly as we schedule them but, as you know, reality is not that way. Therefore, having a flexible and capable team is essential to handling the surprises and fast-moving situations that arise, to be able to capture the opportunities, excel at them, and most importantly, profit from them.

At this point, this common statement about leadership is solved. "It is lonely at the top". That is a false statement now. It is not lonely at the top because you brought people along with you. They are there now to talk through things, support, and counsel. These new leaders can share their opinions, thoughts, and directions with you. They are not, and should not be, a yes-person. You can bounce ideas off of each other, challenge the ideas, and create new ones. They can also lift a load of responsibility from your shoulders and carry it for a while. What does this do? It gives you time. You cannot make more time, but someone can give some time by taking a project from you. When you have developed, empowered, and trusted them; you can hand off the project then forget about it. Of course, they will come back to you to report progress, but the day to day they can handle. This gives you time to do other things, such as business development, development of others, or development of yourself. Time, as we know, is precious; we only have so much, and we should not waste it. As my friend Marissa Nehlson says, "Never waste a day." She learned this while in a relationship with the man and love of her life. She only had so many days with her beloved Army Ranger until cancer took his life too soon. As she stayed with him, every minute of every day up until the day he passed, she realized she would never waste another day in her life because you never know how many you will get. Your team can give you time. They allow you to focus on the truly important rather than the urgent.

CHAPTER 11

A Story of Leadership

I n 1988, I stood before a room full of old goats, in the goat locker - the slang name for chief petty officers and their living quarters. It is supposedly because back in the history of the Navy, this is where they used to keep live goats for milk and meat. I had presented myself to the Chief Petty Officers mess onboard the USS Portland LSD-37 as part of a competition to determine who would represent the ship that quarter as its best sailor. They were asking me questions about why I deserved to be the petty officer of the quarter and my thoughts on various naval issues of the day. Then came the question that attracted the attention of even the disinterested goats sitting at the back eating a sandwich.

They asked me, "Do you think women should be permitted to serve on combat ships?" Up until this point, women could only serve on a limited number of support vessels. As you may have guessed by now, I said yes. A disinterested old goat in the back nearly choked on his sandwich. Surprisingly, I began to sweat. But as they say, the toothpaste was out the tube and it does not go back in.

I do not remember all of the "follow up" questions but I explained that I thought that, if given the chance and proving themselves, there is no reason why they could not serve alongside men in combat. The final question is where, I think, they thought they might get me to turn on myself, "Would you serve at war with a female captain?"

"If she came through the ranks, learned the ship, and was able to fight it then yes, I would serve." I answered

I was selected as the petty officer of the quarter.

Leadership is gender neutral. When you have the skills of leadership, you can lead people.

Deborah Lee James, Debbie as she prefers to be called, was a business unit manager at our company when I was running around serving the 10-person team I spoke about before. She was living in Charleston, SC, leading a program to integrate command and control for the Mine Resistant Ambush

Protected (MRAP) vehicles for our troops in Iraq. This is a great story about a vehicle that saved countless lives, which Debbie tells in her book *"Aim High: Chart Your Course and Find Success"*. As you might imagine that program got high attention from the top of the DoD. She and the team did a wonderful job to get the MRAP ready for the fight.

Despite this high-stakes program, on one of her business trips to Washington, DC, she took time to stop in to see me, my team, and our customer. That night, she took the time to break bread with us, which included an intimate conversation with each member of the team not only about the job, but about their lives. She asked them about their families, how being separated was affecting them, and what she could do to help. She handed each of us a gift card as a token of her appreciation for our efforts.

She was professional, authentic, and down to earth, all at the same time.

Debbie's career was far from over. She went on to become only the second woman to serve as the Secretary of the US Air Force. I sat down with Debbie to ask about her leadership. The following is the result of that conversation.

What was your goal as a leader?

My number one goal as a leader has always been to work in, or be part of, an organization where I felt that there was a purpose, an important purpose that went beyond simply me, my feeling of self-worth, or my paycheck. As a leader, I wanted to make a difference in terms of purpose and advancing the ball for people, advancing the ball for the organization. The second goal as a leader was always about the team, it was about coaching people and bringing up the next generation of leaders. I've been in organizations where I've seen micro managers and I've seen people who have been great coaches, and I always wanted to be the great coach, not the micromanager. And the third thing was I wanted to get things done. So, in all organizations, you have goals, you have objectives, and they're to advance the purpose of the organization, obviously, (but also) it's to grow. If you're in business, it's to do better for people, but a greater goal if you're in the government is getting things done and having that body of accomplishment has always been important to me too.

What steps did you take to get there?

I have to be honest; I didn't start life saying I wanted to be a leader. For me, and I think this is the way most people start, you begin by being an individual contributor at whatever your chosen profession is. Maybe it's not even your chosen profession, maybe it's just the job that you get right out of school. I've always tried to do the best I could at whatever the job was that I had at that moment, even if I didn't feel like it was my dream job. I nonetheless wanted to get things done. I wanted that body of accomplishment and I wanted to make a difference, all of those things I talked about. I sort of had that work ethic - working hard and working to build my competencies - that most of us have we go into a new organization when there's a lot we don't know and, if you're young and starting, you have all of your learning from school, but you don't have all those competencies that have to be built up over time. I always had ambition. I think this is important for people have a desire to advance, they have to search out and they have to ask, "How are there ways that I can advance in this organization or this profession?" You have to have that fire in your belly, that ambition to become a leader and, beyond that, I would say it was a series of getting lucky with mentors who helped me along the way and taking on different assignments. One thing leading to the next, and eventually to my first leadership assignment where I was overseeing people. There was a lot of trial and error about how to lead people, but I eventually got some training in this.

How would you define success?

I think I would define success, first of all, as the three things that I began with, do I feel like I made a difference; that there was an important purpose here and was I a good coach; that the people who served under me would view me as a mentor going forward. Are my people ready for the next stage of leadership? Finally, did we achieve our goals or not. I would look back to those three questions to define success and then maybe add in a fourth one that is very personal. Did I enjoy it, and have some fun along the way? Did I like getting out of bed every morning and going and spending that 8, 10, or 12 hours on the job, or whatever might have been required? Do I look back on it fondly as feeling personally fulfilling to me?

Where did you get your start on your leadership journey?

I wanted to be a diplomat, that was plan A. I wanted to be in the Foreign Service, this was my dream. However, when I left school, moved to Washington, and applied to the State Department, I didn't get the acceptance letter that I was hoping for in the mail. Instead, I got a rejection letter, which, of course, was a huge setback in my young life and I thought I was washed up at the ripe old age of 22. Who would have me now and what would I do now? I went into a deep depression for maybe a week or so, but finally pulled myself together, started applying elsewhere, and got rejection after rejection after rejection from other parts of the government. I did want to do policy again, I felt like that was my purpose. That's what I wanted to do. And finally, I just got this one and only offer, which was from the Department of the Army. It was not my interest area at all, but I had had so many rejections and needed a job, so I simply pivoted and threw myself into this one and only offer that I got, did the best that I could, and tried to build competencies over time. This is where I got really lucky because, within three or four months, my eyes started opening to a whole other world that I had never thought of before. That was the US military, and it turned out that the work I was doing was really interesting and I felt purposeful, so back to that point of purpose, just like I believe I would have felt from the State Department, I was feeling purpose in a new area and direction. And I had a great first team that took me under their wing. They were all much older, they were almost all men, many of them were (in) uniform and I've always been, of course, a civilian. So, they were very different from me, but we had camaraderie, they cared and, again, I felt like a solid part of the team almost from the very beginning. And then I had a great first boss who was that important first professional mentor who not only gave me good advice but also opened some doors for me that I could have never opened. He also made some connections that I couldn't have done for myself. From there, one thing led to the next, led to the next, and to the rest of my career. What started to become apparent? It was all military. That was the thread, as it turns out, that has held together or that has linked all my different jobs throughout 20 years, at different times, in the government, and about 18 years in the private sector. It is all related to national security and the military. I always like to tell this to young people in particular because where you start probably won't be where you finish, and that's okay. It's alright to have a dream and continue to pursue it. If that is what your heart and your mind tell you to do, but it's also okay to pivot, so I was a pivoter. And it turned out that the thing I never thought of was the best thing of all for me. So, you just never know what you're going to like until you try it, and you have to be open to new possibilities.

You talk about how the guys in the army helped you and they cared. How did they help you, and were they positive role models?

They coached me and they were patient with me. I was immediately useful to the team because I had good research skills and I had very good writing skills coming right out of school. This is another principle I have: play to your strengths. I was not strong in many ways. I didn't have the competencies or the knowledge about the army and the budgets and the weapon systems and so on. But I had my two strengths; I was a good researcher and a good writer, so they could do the analytics and I would be the one to write it up. I also had a third, that I was very compatible with people, I was sort of a get-along-person, I was always willing to throw in and had a good work ethic and compatibility. So, I was immediately useful to them as a member of the team, but they were also patient with me and helped me build those competencies that I didn't have.

Throughout your career, did you have any negative role models that taught you what not to do?

Yes, you come up with role models on the personal side of life and the professional side and they can be both positive and negative; it pains me to say it, but a negative role model early on was my mother. I learned from my mother how not to be a parent. My mother was a very negative, glass half full, very critical, and had a certain degree of paranoia in her. I look back on it and I think maybe she suffered from an undiagnosed mental illness with the negativity that was always around her. And so, from watching her, I kind of decided I wanted to be a different type of parent when I got the chance to do so. So, that's one example of a negative role model. I've also had wonderful bosses, for the most part, in my life but I've had two kinds of bad bosses. And these were people who had qualities (of) severe micromanagement. They didn't trust the team, and I think that's partly what drove the micromanagement. There was no amount of communication was ever enough, and I think this related maybe back to some insecurities in them. One of them was unethical and was doing some unethical things in the workplace. The other one was not unethical but capricious; would change direction, without segueing the team (so they) understood the why, or what was going on. It would just be like on Monday do this, you do this, you do this, then you deliver your project on Wednesday; well what is that,

that is not right and I don't want that. So we would constantly be walking on pins and needles, these were qualities that had the entire team up in arms all the time. These were qualities that I saw were destructive and didn't want to repeat.

You talked early on about your qualities and your strengths for the Army job; being a researcher, teammate, and good writer. How did that translate, or what were the characteristics of your leadership style that led to your success?

Well, when I got the chance to be a leader it was a lot of trial and error. I thought I knew what to do just instinctively but I didn't, and I didn't have the training. What I'm going to say now is what I've come to believe over time, not necessarily the way I was right out of the gate. What I've tried to do, certainly in more recent years, is be a people-first leader. Leaders are supposed to be visionary. They're supposed to talk about strategy. All of that I believe in too, but you can talk about vision and strategy and technology and organizational constructs, but the whole thing goes to hell if you don't get the people part of your equation right. If you don't set the tone for a collaborative and a team environment, and the coaching that I talked about, and showing the people that you care about them because the people, after all, are going to be the engine behind the strategy, the technology, and the organization. I think that people first attitude is first for me. I would also say being an ethical leader. Don't ever think that just because you're the Secretary of the Air Force or because you're one of the top five in a major corporation, that suddenly you're entitled to things that you're not, that you can cut corners. I've seen too many people do that in government and business, and it has negative consequences 100% of the time, so very important to keep ethics near and dear (to your heart). Be an ethical leader, because you have to be the role model for everybody else who's watching you, and who is hopefully going to follow you. It is key to be very focused on communications as a leader. If you have a vision but you can't articulate or communicate it, if you can't translate it to the people in the workforce, then you're not going to be (very) effective. Your people must understand how they are important to achieving the overall vision and strategy, no matter what their function in the group may be. I place a high value on effective communications and transparency. Transparent communications are not just rah, rah; tell everybody everything is great all the time. No, you have to face challenges head-on, but you also have to do it in a way that inspires people that they can do it, and that they can get over the hurdles. Additionally, that the opportunities that lie beyond are well worth the sacrifice, whatever the difficulties may be ahead.

Who inspired you?

Well, if we go beyond the bosses and things that I knew firsthand, I remember back in the 90s being so inspired by, and I think this still sits with me, Nelson

Mandela who, if you remember, is considered the father of New South Africa. South Africa, which had lived under apartheid for decades, where the minority white population really ruled the majority black population with an iron fist and the divisions of wealth were ridiculous, with the whites having everything and the blacks having almost nothing. Well, Nelson Mandela started his younger years as a freedom fighter, to try to break free from this system, and he was captured and imprisoned for decades. Eventually, he was set free and became president of South Africa and, somehow, he did not look for revenge. He didn't look to take specific vengeance upon the people who had jailed him or the leaders who had done it, nor did he swing hard against the white population but rather, this is somebody who could forgive then move forward, to have a vision for the future, about Africa and this tremendous ability to heal a nation that had been so terribly fractured and I thought to myself, wow, I don't know if I could have done that, I couldn't have forgiven, I couldn't have healed, and moved forward like that. So, that was very inspirational to me.

What was your biggest hurdle, or hurdles, along the path?

Being a young civilian woman in a much older male uniform dominated profession. Being so different than everybody else, being a liberal arts major at SAIC, which was a highly technical workforce and the Air Force was highly technical. I was the leader of a highly technical workforce even though I am not, by training, a technical person. I think if we're going to talk hurdles, these were both positives and negatives for me, that I was always so different. But, then again, the positives of being different is the power of diversity, so you have to figure out how to make it work for you. It comes back to, in my opinion, always understanding what your strengths are and what they are not, you have to be self-aware enough for that. And then you have to bring your strengths to the table and be immediately helpful to the overall team effort. And along the way, build up your competencies in the areas where you are less strong, but first and foremost play to those strengths. Because, if you do, you can immediately be a major team player and member, and you can even lead the team.

What were your most empowering lessons?

I think my most empowering lessons have been bouncing back from a huge setback, or failure or sadness in life. And it's an ability that only some people have. I do not think I had it naturally, but I've worked on it over the years. You have to look for where is positive lining in some of this negativity that you're confronted with because, if you look carefully, you can always find it. After a divorce, for example, and I've been divorced. This is an example of grief and sadness and what went wrong, etc. etc. the shock of it, but you begin first look yourself in the mirror and ask, what have I learned from it. What will I do differently going forward? And you can also start to think about ways that, as sad as this has had made me, maybe it's for the best.

It's that looking for something positive, even in a negative situation, when I had a couple of bad bosses and bad experiences in the private sector. Boy, did that feel bad at the time. I couldn't wait to get away from it, my stomach was churning, and it was just not an easy time in life. And yet, when I finally did get away from it and was able to look back a little bit with some perspective, I was able to find some positive lessons learned from either people that I consider to this day to still be my friends that I keep in touch with, or it might have been things that I learned in each area, which have helped me since. The most empowering lessons, I think, are finding something positive in negative situations and bouncing back from failure or sadness.

What is one failure you recall and how did you overcome it?

Alright, so let's go back to the bad boss situations. I can't look back at these two short term jobs and say "Wow, I made a huge difference and I brought up the next generation and I got things done." I can't say that. They were brief and I just remember they were stomach-churning events, pretty much. Were they failures, were they the wrong fit that? Yes, the answer is they were, they were all of the above. First of all, what do you do when you are faced with something like this? Well, the first thing I try to do is look myself in the mirror and I try to say, all right, what piece of this was I responsible for. Before you start blaming somebody else or finger-pointing, let's point the finger at me. These were my first jobs out of government, and I was going through a transition period which, let's face it, it's always hard, and the private sector is very different from the government. And maybe I wasn't at the top of my performance. Maybe I was still learning. And by the way, I think it's also important to understand what drives different difficult people, because people learn in different ways. Some people like to be told things verbally others want it in writing. Maybe I didn't try hard enough to confirm the direction of these bosses, and maybe that was part of why I kept getting whipsawed.

However, I did go back subsequently and try to confirm things in writing that had been told to me verbally I did some of that mirror looking and accepting responsibility and pivoting and trying to do things differently, while I was still there. But at the end of the day, it didn't work, and I was still in this stomach-churning situation where, as I said, one of these bosses was severely micromanaging. He was the one who was still carrying the big title and the big salary and yet he wasn't doing the work anymore. And I think that made him very insecure which, by the way, is another principle. If you can understand, as best as you can, what drives difficult people; understand what their pressures are, what their insecurities might be. It won't change them, but it will hopefully change your mindset that you won't take it so personally and feel like it's all on you. And then the last thing you do to overcome something like this, is you do your work as best you can. But you start to look for your next opportunity. And when you find it, you move on with as much positivity and grace and learning from this previous bad situation as you can take. The positive learning is important because nobody likes a Debbie Downer. In the new job, nobody wants to hear about how awful the old job was, so move on with that positivity and grace to the next thing and learn from whatever this bad thing was.

What was the hardest thing you had to learn about yourself?

As I have said, I am a people first person. I also admitted I didn't exactly start that way so, when I was still an individual contributor and working on Capitol Hill, I wasn't managing people but was in an area where I was expected to sort of put together teams and action groups, which required me to influence. So, they weren't directly reporting to me, but I was pulling things together and influencing. My nickname back in those days was "sledge", which was short for sledgehammer because I was considered, shall we say, a little bit out there, a little bit hard. I remember taking the Myers Brigg Personality Indicator, early on. I don't know if you're a fan of that, but I remember distinctly I tested out as an ESTJ, which is extroverted, sensing, thinking, and judging. So, I want to focus on the S, sensing, which means focusing on facts and details, rather than ideas and concepts. Well, after the Capitol Hill experience, I then went to the Pentagon. This was my first time where I was the leader of a team and it wasn't just a few people, it was 180 people and I was giving public speeches and I was responsible for the really big stuff and this really big team and, as I mentioned earlier, I've never done it before, so it was trial and error I made mistakes. I had to go back and redo things. And beyond that, I've been a leader ever since. So, more recently, within the last five years, I retook the Myers Brigg, and I'm no longer, as it turns out, an ESTJ. Now, I'm an ENTJ, and n is the difference and that stands for intuitive. That means I'm now focusing more on ideas and concepts, rather than simply facts and details. And what I believe about this, and what the examiner told me, is that I have mellowed when it came to people issues, the ideas and concepts which, in this case, would be that I'm all about the people now you realize that people make the whole thing go round. It's not just what does the data say, you've got to also understand how people feel, how did the people perceive this. And so, I tell that story because I look back on it. It is also hard for me to believe that "I" was difficult for people or I was hard on people. I used to laugh at that nickname of sledge because I always thought "Gosh, I'm such an easygoing person, you know I don't even know how this whole thing started". But sometimes that's the value of these personality tests, the value of 360-degree reviews that many companies and government agencies do nowadays. It's because you get feedback on yourself, that you can't necessarily see for yourself, we all have some blind spots and it's important, if we want to be good leaders, that we are willing to take that feedback and take it on board and try to do better.

Thank you very much, Debbie, for your time, I am incredibly grateful for this interview and contribution. I was just sitting here thinking what a remarkable life you have had so far, and it is not over yet.

I am not six feet under and still looking to have some fun, live with purpose, coach people; thank you Mark.

After I conducted the interview, I had three takeaways.

1. Put people first, they are the engine that makes everything go.

2. Find a mentor that can help you, guide you, and be your sounding board.

3. Act with humility, like when she realized, "I had to point the finger at myself too."

As you read through this interview, the skills, concepts, tenets, and challenges of leadership are displayed. Secretary James spoke of many of the topics I discussed in the previous chapters. I want to ask you what are your three takeaways?

Again, I encourage you to read her book, "Aim High, Chart Your Course and Find Success"; you will find you have more in common with her, a great leader, than you might think. Follow her example to your leadership success.

The overarching theme from Secretary James's strategy to leadership is to serve the organization that she works within, represents, and guides. I am able to see the message of what "we" have to do, how can we do it, and how can I do my part to make it happen. That is a leader's mindset. I also see how she talked about the ability to play to her strengths, which you must know yourself well to do, and finally how relationships were key to success and failure. In these points, Debbie and I are aligned, as you have read in the previous chapters.

Lastly, she talked about where she received mentorship and training at her first leadership position. She learned from those who went before her. It is key to remember those who walked the path before have answers and wisdom to share with us.

CHAPTER 12

Apply it to Your Life

I remember struggling to keep up. Each day that passed, I could see deadlines coming closer and closer, but the production of the team was not enough to make them. I extended my days from eight to 12 to 16 hours, but the situation was not getting any better. I had four teammates that were not going to have a job soon, if I did not figure a way to increase production. And soon.

I went to talk to my manager, Larry. I told him about the situation and, remarkably, he was not as worried as I wanted him to be. Why was he not freaking out like I was? He listened and asked questions and nodded and said, "I see", a few times.

I told him how much I was doing to make this a success, to make it profitable, and keep our clients.

When I was done with my explanation, he asked me the question he was probably waiting to ask. "What are your people doing while you are working 16-hour days, are they working with you?" Not very confidently, I said no. Why not? Was his next question, I could feel this going somewhere but I was not liking the direction of this wind. I almost did not want to answer him. But I said because they do not know as much as I do. "Who is at fault for that?" I knew the answer, but I did not want to admit it. I tried to say they went to school, training, they have a degree, this and that, but he repeated the question again and again. Finally, I relented. After I picked up my shattered ego off the floor and brushed it aside, I was ready to admit I had failed the team and then hear the solution he was to offer.

Shockingly, it involved me. (Yes, I am being facetious). I had to change, and fast. I began to coach the team, teach them, encourage them, and support them. They began to thrive, and we made all the deadlines.

I had failed to lead. And we almost paid for it, dearly. But when I changed, when I pointed at myself, as Debbie says, and as Larry made me see; then things changed. That is how it works, when you change, the things around you change. It seemed hard at the time.

119

But looking back on it, it was not that hard. I first had to change my mindset. I had to stop focusing on me, stop having the team serve me, and understanding that it was not all about my production, but our production. I began to focus on them, how can I help them produce, succeed, learn and grow? I met with them regularly during each day, teaching them at first, coaching them, and, most importantly, encouraging them. I held them accountable for their part of the team too. I made sure they understood that they were needed for us to succeed. This is absolutely, without a doubt true. No one wins alone. I needed them.

Start today. You can make a difference in every aspect of your life. The tide raises all boats. When your leadership, the tide, gets better, those around you will get better. When those around you get better, those around them get better, and so on. Your better leadership will have multiplying affect beyond your reach. When you follow the steps of this book, develop your people to be leaders, then they will develop their people to be leaders. You and them, will begin to change the world.

You are not that much different than me, we share the same desire to be better tomorrow than we are today, to succeed, and be happy. When we keep striving forward each day, we can go a long way. The key is to keep going. Of course, there will be setbacks, obstacles, hurdles, and failures. But keep going anyway. Champions are not the ones who have it the easiest or are the most talented. The champions are the ones who never quit and kept going.

You see, I have not always had all the answers. I had mentors, coaches, and other leaders along the way that helped me. You do not have to have all the answers. What you need to have is a willingness to learn, be open to suggestions and constructive criticism, and have the humility to admit failure then change course. If you can do this, you will develop a belief in yourself that will be unshakeable, and you will be able to take on most anything. Even better is that you will be able to transfer belief to your people. This may be the single most important thing you can do for them. But you must believe first, you cannot give away what you do not possess.

If you were to take a poll of people today, and they answered honestly about their level of belief in themselves, you might be surprised by how low it is. All people have challenges. It is the leader that, despite the challenges, exudes and displays belief and confidence that we will win. You can be that kind of leader. You are that kind of leader.

If you enjoyed this book, please give it a Five Star Rating from where you purchased it. This will help others enjoy it and gain the fruits that you have.

I have enjoyed writing it and sharing the wisdom I have gained from the past 44 years of leadership. 44 years ago, I never thought I would be sitting here writing a book to help so many people but I am. I want you to be doing the same in your time, I know you can do it and believe you will do far better than I have. I want that for you and expect you will have no trouble doing it.

Good luck, I am behind you.

HOW CAN I HELP YOU?

I am available to speak to your organization, perform workshops, or present a DISC Assessment for you.

To find out more about my services please visit
MarkMissigman.com